LAY WORDS
FOR
LAWYERS

EXPANDED SECOND EDITION

Also by William Drennan

The Fourth Strike: Hiring and Training the Disadvantaged (editor)

Advocacy Words: A Thesaurus

A Modern Holy Land Story

William Drennan

LAY WORDS
FOR
LAWYERS

EXPANDED SECOND EDITION

AMERICAN BAR ASSOCIATION
Solo, Small Firm and
General Practice Division

Cover design by Mary Anne Kulchawik/ABA Publishing.

Printed in the United States of America.

19 18 17 16 15   5 4 3 2 1

Library of Congress Cataloging-in-Publication Data

Drennan, William, 1935-   author.
  Lay words for lawyers : analogies and key words to advance your case and communicate with clients / William Drennan. — Expanded second edition.
      pages cm
  ISBN 978-1-62722-917-3 (softcover : alk. paper) —
  ISBN 978-1-62722-918-0 (e-book)
1. Law--Language. 2. English language—United States—Terms and phrases.
3. Legal composition—Language. 4. Forensic oratory—Language. I. Title.
  KF156.D74 2015
  340'.14—dc23   2014042320

Discounts are available for books ordered in bulk. Special consideration is given to state bars, CLE programs, and other bar-related organizations. Inquire at Book Publishing, ABA Publishing, American Bar Association, 321 N. Clark Street, Chicago, Illinois 60654-7598.

www.ShopABA.org

In memory of my father

Contents

Lay Words by Chapter

Chapter 1:
Computers

- active attack
- Barney page
- cobweb site
- crash
- cul de site
- dog food
- geek out
- Google
- gronk
- information island
- intranet
- netopath
- network meltdown
- orphan page
- out of band
- padded cell
- passive attack
- salami attack
- tiger team
- virus

Chapter 2:
Mature

- Blanchard and Davis
- "Bless This House"
- Bonnie and Clyde
- "Come On-a My House"
- Dagwood Bumstead
- "Dear Hearts and Gentle People"
- Father Chuck O'Malley
- Fred and Ginger
- Hitler
- "I Didn't Know the Gun Was Loaded"
- "It Takes Two to Tango"
- Ivan Shark
- "I've Heard That Song Before"
- Joseph Stalin
- the Lone Ranger
- the "Mad Bomber"
- "Mairzy Doats"
- milquetoast
- Napoleon Bonaparte

- "Pistol-Packin' Mama"
- "Praise the Lord and Pass the Ammunition"
- "Remember Pearl Harbor"
- "September Song"
- "Smoke Gets in Your Eyes"
- "The Sorcerer's Apprentice"
- Stromboli
- "Thanks for the Memories"
- victory gardens
- "the weed of crime bears bitter fruit"
- "Whispering Hope"
- "You Always Hurt the One You Hate"
- "You'd Be So Nice to Come Home To"

Chapter 3:
Boomers

- "Ain't That a Shame"
- Darth Vader
- "Everybody's Somebody's Fool"

- Graceland
- "The Great Pretender"
- Howdy Doody
- "I Can Dream, Can't I?"
- "I Write the Songs"
- John Wayne Gacy
- "Look What They've Done to My Song"
- "May the Truth be with you"
- "My Way"
- "Strangers in the Night"
- "Venus"
- Watergate
- "Your Cheatin' Heart"

Chapter 4:
Generation X

- "Alone"
- the Berlin Wall
- collapse of the Soviet Union
- "Cuts Like a Knife"
- "The Glamorous Life"
- "I'll Be There for You"

Chapter 7:
Literary

- "A man's home is his castle"
- "The mass of men lead lives of quiet desperation"
- "not with a bang but a whimper"
- "The object of torture is torture"
- Orwell on equality
- "Pardon one offense and you encourage the commission of many"
- "Parting is such sweet sorrow"
- Polybius on conscience
- "Power tends to corrupt; absolute power corrupts absolutely"
- "She speaks, yet she says nothing"
- ". . . strength without justice is tyrannical"
- "There's small choice in rotten apples"
- Trojan horse
- "Truth never yet fell dead"

- "Weakness is not in your word"
- ". . . where wealth accumulates, and men decay"
- "You can't make a silk purse out of a sow's ear"
- "You cause what you abuse"

Chapter 8:
Sports

- beanball
- Black Sox
- blitz
- blown save
- bush league
- designated hitter
- get to first base
- left runners in scoring position
- out of left field
- power play
- quarterback
- red zone
- replay
- sacking the quarterback

Preface

It is perhaps a cliché to say that communication is important to human progress. But for the legal profession it is *vital*, the lifeblood on which it is based.

Every discipline has words particular to it, be it medicine, accounting, sociology, a host of other academic disciplines—and law. Attorneys communicate with each other using the language of the profession. They in turn communicate with jurists, and jurists with them and with each other, using the same terms. In a profession hallowed by centuries of enlightened expression, the language of the law is, as it were, etched in verbal stone, part of a literary pantheon.

Enter the layman—the nonlawyer without whose presence there are no cases, without whom the practice of the profession is moot. The layman has his own language—perhaps precise, perhaps not. Yet to pursue a case—to prosecute it, defend it, *win* it—the attorney must understand this language and be able to use it to advance his case.

This expanded second edition of *Lay Words for Lawyers*—with 45 percent more entries than in the first edition—provides verbal ammunition for you to do this. And the armament is meant not to be linguistic buckshot but laser beam—focusing on making a point as efficiently and effectively as possible. Words have been chosen whose mere mention is intended to elicit strong mental—but particularly strong emotional—images or memories in the hearer, to stimulate a flood of associations that will help advance your case.

The terms have been arranged into nine categories. Computers, the first category, has a vocabulary all its own. The next four are based on year of birth: Mature (1930–1945), Boomers (1946–1964), Generation X (1965–1977), and Generation Y (1978–1996). Clearly there is some overlap between or even among generations; the terms have been placed in the category that most closely applies to, or that came into prominence during, that generation. Thus, for example, a song released in the late sixties, even though this is during the Generation X birth years (1965–1977), more appropriately applies to the Boomers (born 1946–1964). However, the next category, Pangenerational, truly covers all the generations; the terms here would be known equally, or close to equally, by all. The Literary chapter presents expressions from classic works. The next category, Sports, like Computers, has its own unique terms. And the final category, Millennial, features terms that have come to prominence since the start of the third millennium.

Mature counsel need to know vocabularies used by, for example, Generation X or Generation Y clients. Young attorneys could profit by knowing, for instance, World War II analogies when addressing Mature jurors. And all can benefit by knowing the language of computer literacy.

Whether you are speaking with your client, addressing the jury, or questioning a witness, you need to know words that are significant to them—words they use and words that *you* can use to advance your case. Let *Lay Words for Lawyers* help you to do this.

Acknowledgments

My thanks particularly to the following in getting this book into print and published:

To Richard G. Paszkiet, Director, ABA Entity Book Content Publishing, who expertly guided it to publication.

To my wife, Christina, for her continued support.

A Note to the Reader

The terms "he" and "she," "him" and "her," and "his" and "hers" are used interchangeably in this book. The age ranges for members of the generational groups included in this book (Mature, Boomers, Generation X, and Generation Y) are as of 2014.

This book is designed to provide accurate and authoritative information in regard to the subject matter covered with the understanding that the author is not engaged in rendering expert legal or other professional services. If legal advice or other expert assistance is required, the services of a competent professional should be sought.

Any use of the information in this book is at the reader's discretion. The author and publisher specifically disclaim any and all liability arising directly or indirectly from the use or application of any information contained in this book.

While every effort has been made to collate, check, and present without ambiguity all information contained herein, the variety of sources from which they have been assembled and differing methods of reporting render verification oftentimes impossible. Thus they are published without warranty.

All the examples in the "Example" section for each entry in this book are hypothetical and do not refer to any actual cases or proceedings.

About the Author

William Drennan is president and editorial director of Drennan Communications, consultants in verbal and written communication, drenlit@earthlink.net. In a literary career spanning five decades, Mr. Drennan, a native New Yorker, has served as author, consultant, editor, copy editor, and agent. He is the author of *Advocacy Words: A Thesaurus*, published by the American Bar Association and now in its expanded third edition. He and his wife, Christina, are parents of Caroline and William and grandparents of Liam, Aubrey, Harper, and Ian.

LAY WORDS
FOR
LAWYERS

EXPANDED SECOND EDITION

Chapter 1

Computers

■ active attack

Client/juror/witness age range: Any age, but especially younger clients, jurors, and witnesses.

Explanation: A network intrusion to change or delete information.

Application: To establish the specific meaning of the term.

Example: "Our computer privacy was violated. Data were scrambled or eliminated completely. It came under active attack."

■ Barney page

Client/juror/witness age range: Any age, but especially younger clients, jurors, and witnesses.

Explanation: A Web page that is developed quickly in response to a fast-developing situation.

Application: To understand what a client or witness means in explaining, for example, why he or she covered a story in a certain way.

Example: "I had to move fast. I had to get eyewitnesses, statements. It was almost like I was doing a Barney page on the run."

■ cobweb site

Client/juror/witness age range: Any age, but especially younger clients, jurors, and witnesses.

Explanation: A website that has not been updated for a long time.

Application: To establish negligence in failing to maintain standards, such as safety precautions.

Example: "[The defendant's] plant was unsafe, not up to mandated safety standards. In computer terms, it was a cobweb site."

■ crash

Client/juror/witness age range: Any age, but especially younger clients, jurors, and witnesses.

Explanation: To cease to function effectively.

Application: Can be applied to mitigate guilt when one's client is depressed and/or has suffered severe reverses in life.

Example: In, for example, a trial's penalty phase: "Bear in mind that even though you have found [my client] guilty of manslaughter, his life was overwhelmed with problems: He had lost his job, his wife had left him, and the bank was foreclosing on his house. In computer terms, his life had crashed."

■ cul de site

Client/juror/witness age range: Any age, but especially younger clients, jurors, and witnesses.

Explanation: A website that has useless or no links.

Application: To understand what a client or witness means in explaining why he or she left a particular job or situation.

Example: "Well, counselor, the job was a dead end. I was going nowhere. It was like a cul de site."

■ dog food

Client/juror/witness age range: Any age, but especially younger clients, jurors, and witnesses.

Explanation: A computer term denoting testing of software on the manufacturer's staff before marketing.

Application: To establish that due care was taken before something was done.

Example: "[My client] took great care before marketing his product. To use a computer term, he decided to—and did—dog food *on his own staff* before releasing it for distribution."

■ geek out

Client/juror/witness age range: Any age, but especially younger clients, jurors, and witnesses.

Explanation: Talking about computing matters socially.

Application: To establish the meaning of the term.

Example: "We didn't attack their programs. They told us themselves. Or, specifically, one of their guys did. He had a few drinks and really geeked out at a party."

■ Google

Client/juror/witness age range: Any age, but especially younger clients, jurors, and witnesses.

Explanation: A widely used search engine.

Application: To establish, by mere mention that this search engine has been used, that comprehensive research has been done in a given matter.

Example: "My client exercised due diligence in researching this matter for his company. He Googled all the relevant factors thoroughly."

■ gronk

Client/juror/witness age range: Any age, but especially younger clients, jurors, and witnesses.

Explanation: A computer that isn't working.

Application: To establish the meaning of the term.

Example: "After the hackers got into our system, our computer doesn't work. It has become a gronk."

▪ information island

Client/juror/witness age range: Any age, but especially younger clients, jurors, and witnesses.

Explanation: Data not online.

Application: To establish the meaning of the term, particularly in regard to the data's general availability.

Example: "I have researched the background of this subject thoroughly using search engines, but the real authority is [name the expert]. He has considerable material, but none of it is online. It's really on an information island."

▪ intranet

Client/juror/witness age range: Any age, but especially younger clients, jurors, and witnesses.

Explanation: A self-contained network not accessible to those outside the network.

Application: To establish the meaning of the term, particularly regarding information accessibility.

Example: "It's a very close-mouthed organization. They reveal very little outside the company. They have their own intranet, and a lot of their secrets remain secrets there."

▨ netopath

Client/juror/witness age range: Any age, but especially younger clients, jurors, and witnesses.

Explanation: A network stalker or other extreme abuser.

Application: To establish the meaning of the term.

Example: "He won't let me alone. First it was phone calls. Then I got an unlisted number. Now he's sending me threatening e-mail. He's a real netopath."

▨ network meltdown

Client/juror/witness age range: Any age, but especially younger clients, jurors, and witnesses.

Explanation: A computer network overload because of heavy user activity resulting in delayed response time.

Application: To create stress on a government agency, company, or other organization, with the implication that it could have been avoided with appropriate preplanning.

Example: "The response time to this [emergency, disaster, accident, etc.] could have been considerably shortened if [the defendant, respondent, etc.] had taken the proper precautions. But in computer terms, it was nothing less than a network meltdown."

▣ orphan page

Client/juror/witness age range: Any age, but especially younger clients, jurors, and witnesses.

Explanation: A page on a website not linked to any other page and that generally is unknown.

Application: To establish isolation as a factor of use in a client's case.

Example: "My client should not be denied benefits simply because he didn't know they were available. He is elderly, blind, and lives out in the country. To draw a computer analogy, his isolated situation was like that of an orphan page."

▣ out of band

Client/juror/witness age range: Any age, but especially younger clients, jurors, and witnesses.

Explanation: Any communication not e-mail-based.

Application: To establish the meaning of the term.

Example: "I talked to [the defendant], but it was over the phone. Sometimes he sends snail mail, but never e-mail. He's really out of band."

padded cell

Client/juror/witness age range: Any age, but especially younger clients, jurors, and witnesses.

Explanation: Software that limits use of a computer or network.

Application: By extension, any use-limiting rule or procedure.

Example: "This defendant was given limited access to his employer's files, but he violated that restriction to steal information. Computerists call such restrictions a padded cell. We submit that this defendant should learn about another type of cell, this one not padded."

passive attack

Client/juror/witness age range: Any age, but especially younger clients, jurors, and witnesses.

Explanation: Spying on a computer network without changing the data.

Application: A shorthand term familiar to computerists to summarize the nature of this theft of intellectual property.

Example: "[The respondent] accessed private patent data from some of our transmission lines without our permission. It was nothing less than a passive attack."

salami attack

Client/juror/witness age range: Any age, but especially younger clients, jurors, and witnesses.

Explanation: An attack on a computer network that involves switching small amounts of money or other assets from one account to another.

Application: A shorthand term for such transfers, it can be applied to any surreptitious switching, whether computer-related or not.

Example: "The defendant switched small amounts of money under various guises, such as 'service charges,' and put the funds into his own account. Computerists call this a 'salami attack,' because the amounts sliced are so small. But there is another name for it: thievery."

tiger team

Client/juror/witness age range: Any age, but especially younger clients, jurors, and witnesses.

Explanation: A gang of hackers who probe a network's weaknesses.

Application: By extension, any spying attack.

Example: "My client hired these people in good faith. He didn't know that they were there to spy on his company. They were, in computer parlance, a tiger team, intent on learning privileged information from his computer and other files."

■ virus

Client/juror/witness age range: Any age, but especially younger clients, jurors, and witnesses.

Explanation: A malicious program that enters a computer and infects files.

Application: By extension, this term, along with its biological equivalent, can be used to describe any malicious act that spreads.

Example: "This defendant wasn't content with corrupting one youngster. He seduced all of this boy's friends with his crack cocaine. Think of a computer virus or a biological virus. Both can be lethal. Here, the defendant was spreading nothing less than a drug-dealing virus."

Chapter 2

Mature

Born 1930–1945

■ Blanchard and Davis

Client/juror/witness age range: 69–84

Explanation: All-American football players Felix ("Doc") Blanchard, a fullback, and Glenn Davis, a halfback, were the well-known stars of the undefeated Army (West Point) team from 1944 to 1946.

Application: Citable as examples of excellent individual performance to achieve a group's goals.

Example: "[My clients'] record in managing [a company in question] was exemplary. They worked hard together for the company as a whole. To use a 1940s college football analogy, they were the Blanchard and Davis of the [name it] industry."

■ "Bless This House"

Client/juror/witness age range: 69–84

Explanation: A hymn that asks God's blessing on one's home.

Application: To portray the robbery or burglary of one's house as not merely the loss of property but also the defilement of one's house.

Example: "The defendant did more than just [rob or burglarize] this family's house. He raped it. All their private, personal, precious things have been pawed

14

through as if they were just junk to be peddled on the street. Their home—*their home*—has been defiled. There was a lovely hymn written years ago, called 'Bless This House.' It asks God to bless those who dwell within and to keep want and trouble out. Perhaps in your heart you will join with me in asking God to bless this house, to make it clean again."

Bonnie and Clyde

Client/juror/witness age range: 69–84

Explanation: Bonnie Elizabeth Parker and Clyde Chestnut Barrow were notorious American criminals in the early 1930s.

Application: To demonstrate that crime patterns continue but are updated for modern times.

Example: "The criminal couple on trial here never left home to break the law. They hacked into hundreds of accounts, stripping people of their savings, sometimes their life's savings. There was another couple years ago, Bonnie and Clyde. Maybe you heard of them. They even made a movie about them. Bonnie and Clyde and their gang went on a crime spree in the early 1930s in this country before they were stopped. Now, the two before you here are just latter-day Bonnie and Clydes. But instead of breaking into banks, they ravaged people's accounts twenty-first-century style—from the comfort of their computers."

■ "Come On-a My House"

Client/juror/witness age range: 69–84

Explanation: A popular song of the early 1950s that talks about the benefits of going to a particular house.

Application: The title of this song can be used to refer to illegal activities at a particular location.

Example: "The defendant enticed children to come to his 'house,' actually his place of business. Remember the song 'Come On-a My House' from the 1950s? Well, that was the defendant's approach, but instead of giving the children candy, as in the song, he sold them crack cocaine!"

■ Dagwood Bumstead

Client/juror/witness age range: 69–84

Explanation: A main character in the long-running and continuing comic strip *Blondie* and, principally in the 1940s, also on radio and in film. Dagwood was well-meaning but bumbling and often shouldn't be taken seriously.

Application: To show that someone chronically prone to mistakes should be allowed some leeway in assessing guilt.

Example: "My client is accused of making erroneous, slanderous statements. However, you should know that he is more than a bit of a clown, and he often gets things wrong. Some of you will remember Dagwood Bumstead, from the comic strip *Blondie* and also in the movies and on radio. Dogwood was eccentric—remember the gargantuan 'Dagwood sandwich'?—outlandish, and prone to blunders, but he was also a generous but gullible person. That's my client—this good man often speaks before he thinks, and I ask that you keep this in mind as we proceed in this case."

◼ "Dear Hearts and Gentle People"

Client/juror/witness age range: 69–84

Explanation: A sentimental song that extols the virtues of a safe life among people one trusts.

Application: To contrast a contented life in a safe community with a violent, criminal intrusion.

Example: "The victims in this case were enjoying a happy, quiet evening at home. You know, there was a song some years ago called 'Dear Hearts and Gentle People.' Maybe some of you remember it. The lyrics go on to say, 'who live in my hometown.' That was the case for this family. Then these defendants, a gang of bikers passing through, assaulted this family and robbed them. 'Dear hearts'? 'Gentle people'? I'll tell you what these thugs are: criminals!"

■ Father Chuck O'Malley

Client/juror/witness age range: 69–84

Explanation: A fictional priest played by Bing Crosby in the films *Going My Way* (Academy Award, Best Actor, 1944) and *The Bells of St. Mary's* (1945). Father Chuck was easygoing and permissive but compassionate and with a strong moral code. He worked with children and adolescents creatively and constructively, with no hint of impropriety.

Application: Could be effective in defending a priest or other clergyperson wrongly accused of sexual or other crimes.

Example: "Do you remember Father Chuck O'Malley in *Going My Way* and *The Bells of St. Mary's*? That's [my client]."

■ Fred and Ginger

Client/juror/witness age range: 69–84

Explanation: Fred Astaire and Ginger Rogers were a dance pair who made ten films together from 1933 to 1949.

Application: To show how intraproject teamwork benefited an organization.

Example: "As CFO and COO, respectively, my clients made this company run. Their efforts meshed beautifully to produce success after success. Remember the dance team of Fred Astaire and Ginger Rogers in their great movies of the thirties and forties? Businesswise, that was how my clients worked, with the sum, in effect, greater than its parts."

■ Hitler

Client/juror/witness age range: Adolf Hitler is known to all generations in this book, but this entry is included in the Mature group because a significant number of this group were alive during that era and remember when he was in the news constantly.

Explanation: The most notorious criminal of the twentieth century, who, as dictator of Germany, authorized the murder of millions of innocent victims.

Application: To compare Hitler's actions with the predations of contemporary drug gang lords or other criminal leaders.

Example: "This defendant stopped at nothing—*nothing*—to achieve his ends. Murder, torture—anything to enhance his drug empire. He is in fact a drug lord Hitler, utterly ruthless and contemptuous of human life."

■ "I Didn't Know the Gun Was Loaded"

Client/juror/witness age range: 69–84

Explanation: A well-known song of the late 1940s and early '50s, its lyrics express a none-too-sincere "apology" by the shooter to the victim.

Application: To confirm that one is responsible for use of a lethal weapon in his possession.

Example: "The defendant, an adult, claims he didn't know there were bullets in his father's old gun. Well, there was a song years ago called 'I Didn't Know the Gun Was Loaded.' The lyrics go on to say, 'And I'm so sorry, my friend.' That excuse is as lame as the one in this case. The shooter had a responsibility to know."

■ "It Takes Two to Tango"

Client/juror/witness age range: 69–84

Explanation: A popular song of the early 1950s, it says that a partnership (in the song's case, romantic) doesn't work unless both parties are involved in it.

Application: To help establish that one of the people in the partnership (for example, in business or a marriage) failed to fulfill his or her responsibilities.

Example: "[The respondent] reneged on his responsibilities under this business partnership agreement. He shared the profits but not the work. Remember the song 'It Takes Two to Tango'? Well, it does take two, but [the respondent] left [the plaintiff] to dance with the work alone!"

Ivan Shark

Client/juror/witness age range: 69–84

Explanation: The evil mastermind in the 1939–1949 radio adventure series *Captain Midnight*.

Application: To highlight the illegal support of international as well as domestic crime.

Example: "The defendant before us is responsible for the death and maiming of thousands of innocent people in fomenting, then dealing arms for, wars large and small around the globe. Some of you may remember Ivan Shark, the vicious nemesis of Captain Midnight on the radio during the World War II era. Shark and his sadistic daughter, Fury, along with their henchmen, used any means necessary to cut deals with and otherwise support the Axis powers as well as criminals in this country. This defendant is a twenty-first-century version of Shark and should be removed from civilized society."

■ "I've Heard That Song Before"

Client/juror/witness age range: 69–84

Explanation: A 1940s song that brings back memories.

Application: To counter a defendant's counsel's excuse to explain away his client's behavior.

Example: "The defendant cites his rough life to excuse his criminal acts. There was a song in the 1940s called 'I've Heard That Song Before.' Some of you might remember it. Helen Forrest made it with Harry James. That was right after the Depression, when *everyone* had it rough but *still* took responsibility for their actions. Well, Mr. Defendant, we've heard *your* song before, and it's *no excuse!*"

■ Joseph Stalin

Client/juror/witness age range: 69–84

Explanation: Joseph Stalin, born Iosef Vissarionovich Dzhugashvili, was the leader—in effect, dictator—of the Soviet Union from the mid-1920s until his death in 1953. He presided over a regime that murdered millions of people who opposed—or even simply did not support—his rule.

Application: To accuse a defendant of using Stalinist methods of rule over an organization.

Example: "The defendant before us was dictator of a criminal empire that used any means at their disposal to achieve their ends—child prostitution, murder, drug dealing, terrorist financing, and money laundering—to name just a few. Some of you will remember Joseph Stalin, the dictator of the Soviet Union who murdered millions of people in his notorious purges to expand and consolidate his power. Well, the guy on trial here today is a latter-day Stalin—a vicious, ruthless wharf rat with nothing but contempt for human life."

the Lone Ranger

Client/juror/witness age range: 62–84 (i.e., overlap with some Boomer years)

Explanation: The fictional "daring and resourceful masked rider of the Plains who, with his faithful Indian companion, Tonto, led the fight for law and order in the early western United States" (according to announcer Fred Foy) was on radio from 1933 to 1954 and on television from 1949 to 1957.

Application: To draw a parallel between a fighter for urban justice and the noble, legendary Lone Ranger.

Example: "My client has worked tirelessly to prevent the slumlords who have brought these baseless charges against him from exploiting and even evicting the urban poor from the hovels they rent out. Those older among you will remember the Lone Ranger from radio and television. He constantly strove to make our early West a safer, more decent place from outlaws. And just as the Lone Ranger defeated Butch Cavendish and his gang and other evildoers, I now urge you to reject the claims of this gang of urban exploiters."

■ the "Mad Bomber"

Client/juror/witness age range: 69–84

Explanation: George Metesky, dubbed the "Mad Bomber" by the media, was a mentally unbalanced man who planted numerous bombs in New York in the 1940s and 1950s that injured several people.

Application: To show that extenuating circumstances—in this case, mental illness—can affect how the judicial system deals with offenders.

Example: "My client admits what he did—he had been fired from his job, and then took what he thought was revenge by planting some bombs at the company's headquarters and later by trying to burn the building down. Some people were injured. He has been diagnosed as a paranoid schizophrenic. This case virtually mirrors that of George Metesky, the so-called Mad Bomber. Some of you may remember that he had a grudge against a local public utility and then retaliated by planting several bombs in public places in New York in the 1940s and 1950s that injured a number of people. He was sent to a facility for the criminally insane.

"My client is not a terrorist with an international political agenda. He is a mentally unbalanced person who desperately needs help, and we ask that he be sent to a place where his illness can be treated until he can return to society as a productive member."

■ "Mairzy Doats"

Client/juror/witness age range: 69–84

Explanation: A "nonsense" song ("Mairzy Doats" = "Mares Eat Oats") popular in the 1940s.

Application: Could be effective in defending a person given to glib, inaccurate statements that may have gotten him into trouble.

Example: "[My client] is simply a free spirit—not given to precise statements, like lawyers [this might generate some constructive laughter]. To him, the song 'Mairzy Doats'—remember that, in the 1940s?—made perfect sense."

■ milquetoast

Client/juror/witness age range: 69–84

Explanation: A weak, ineffectual person. The word is derived from Caspar Milquetoast, the henpecked husband in *The Timid Soul*, a comic strip by

H. T. Webster that ran in the *New York World* and later the *New York Herald Tribune* from 1924 to 1952.

Application: To show that one is responsible for his own actions, even if subject to harassment.

Example: "Remember Caspar Milquetoast, the weak-willed man whose wife, Vi, constantly nagged him in the funnies [comic strips] some years ago? Well, we have another milquetoast before us now—the defendant—but this guy is in real trouble. His wife ran a drug-dealing racket right out of their house. She ordered him to make the exchanges and he did—he didn't have the guts to face up to her.

"His wife will face justice herself, but meanwhile, send this complicit coward—this milquetoast—to prison, where the staff will give him plenty more orders—these ones legal—to obey."

■ Napoleon Bonaparte

Client/juror/witness age range: 69–84

Explanation: The French emperor whose 1812 invasion of Russia was, to a significant degree, defeated by the Russian winter.

Application: To show that might does not always prevail in a conflict.

Example: "On trial here is a man whose constitutional rights have been violated by an arrogant, insensitive, callous central government that has used all its coercive powers to try to crush him. A man who has a public defender because he can't afford a lawyer. But might doesn't always make right. You'll remember in history that Napoleon Bonaparte's mighty army was defeated in its 1812 invasion of Russia not by force but, basically, by nature itself—the Russian winter, which stopped the army's advance and caused numerous deaths. In this case, make this a lesson learned—stifle the mighty judicial army of the state by the snows of justice!"

■ "Pistol-Packin' Mama"

Client/juror/witness age range: 69–84

Explanation: A popular song of the 1940s, it talks of a gun-wielding woman who is prepared to use it.

Application: To help establish guilt in a woman who carried a firearm and used it in a criminal way.

Example: "This was not a crime of passion. The defendant armed herself beforehand. Remember that 1940s song 'Pistol-Packin' Mama'? Well, this mama didn't 'lay that pistol down,' as the song pleads, but used it to murder her [husband, lover, victim, etc.]!"

■ "Praise the Lord and Pass the Ammunition"

Client/juror/witness age range: 69–84

Explanation: A song popular during World War II that asserted a moral basis for conducting a war against evil forces.

Application: To make a connection between military activities in World War II—universally considered a "just" war—and similar antiterrorist activities today, particularly by someone accused of using excessive force.

Example: "[My client] is accused of not using sufficient 'restraint' as a military man fighting terrorists overseas. But he was guided by the same moral principle that inspired 'the Greatest Generation' in World War II: 'praise the Lord and pass the ammunition.'"

■ "Remember Pearl Harbor"

Client/juror/witness age range: 69–84

Explanation: The principal motivational exhortation to the general public in the United States during World War II.

Application: To establish remembrance as an important element in combating evil.

Example: "You know, memory can be an important factor when we seek to do right, and it is in the case before us. Some of you will remember the expression 'Remember Pearl Harbor' after the sneak attack there by Japan on Sunday morning, December 7, 1941. The attack triggered our entry into World War II, and the exhortation inspired our nation to work toward final victory. In the case here, the modus operandi by the defendant was sickeningly similar to that of the aggressor on December 7. He waited until he thought his victim was most vulnerable, and then he slashed her repeatedly until he ran off. I simply ask: Remember the evidence. Send this defendant to his punishment, as the vicious attack of December 7 was ultimately punished."

■ "September Song"

Client/juror/witness age range: Principally Mature (69–84), but its compassionate message also can resonate with younger people.

Explanation: A wistful song about a peaceful old age.

Application: Usable to contrast sensitive treatment of older people with insensitive policies of, for example, some nursing homes.

Example: "Don't close this nursing home. For many of its residents, this is all they have. For many, their only friends are here. Some seniors among you might remember 'September Song,' which was introduced some years ago in a Broadway play by a gentleman named Walter Huston. For those younger, it tells of an aging man's hope to live his final days contentedly. The residents of this nursing home deserve as much. For them, as the song says, the days are dwindling down to a precious few. Don't put them out on the street."

■ "Smoke Gets in Your Eyes"

Client/juror/witness age range: 69–84

Explanation: A Jerome Kern song featured in the Broadway musical and later film *Roberta*.

Application: A caution to jurors not to be fooled by opposing counsel's arguments.

Example: "Opposing counsel has used the evidence to weave a tale to try to prop up [his client's] position. Some years ago the composer Jerome Kern wrote the song 'Smoke Gets in Your Eyes'—about how emotions can fool you, if you let them. But don't let evidence smoke get in your eyes in this case. Don't be fooled by opposing counsel's siren song."

■ "The Sorcerer's Apprentice"

Client/juror/witness age range: Principally Mature (69–84), but this classic story spans the generations.

Explanation: A sorcerer's apprentice who knows how to turn magic on but not how to turn it off.

Application: As a mitigating factor when a young employee—or anyone new and experienced—gets into a problem that balloons out of control because he or she lacks the experience to cope with it.

Example: "My young client—he's just a teenager—knew there was a problem when his terminal crashed. But he didn't know that he had inadvertently triggered a domino effect that shut down all the store's terminals for the better part of a day. He meant well, and he tried his best. I can't help thinking of Mickey as the Sorcerer's Apprentice in Disney's *Fantasia*. Remember that? Mickey could turn the spell on, but he didn't know how to turn it off. The sorcerer had never told him. Well, it's kind of the same here. The store [name the employer] had never instructed him on how to deal with a computer crisis such as this. Don't penalize him. Give him another chance."

▪ Stromboli

Client/juror/witness age range: 69–84

Explanation: In Disney's 1940 film *Pinocchio*, the sleazy showman who threatens to harm Pinocchio.

Application: To show how the strong and coercive exploit the weak and helpless.

Example: "This defendant here, who is a pimp as well as a drug dealer, used runaway teenage girls for his prostitution racket and then got them on drugs. You might remember Disney's movie *Pinocchio*, where the evil showman Stromboli kidnaps the defenseless and innocent Pinocchio, threatens to force him into his show, and then says, 'And when you are growing too old, you will make good firewood!' Well, here we're talking about real people. When the girls became too sick, or too addicted, or too beaten up to continue, he literally threw them out on the street. I urge you to send this repulsive creature to prison, where he can try to exploit the walls of his cell."

■ "Thanks for the Memories"

Client/juror/witness age range: 69–84

Explanation: The theme song of longtime comedian Bob Hope. The song itself is not humorous but wistful, nostalgic, and gentle. The title has entered the mainstream as a "thank you" line for a career well served or even a lifetime well lived.

Application: It establishes the basic character of a client who, later in a career or in life, has been accused or even found guilty in a legal action after an otherwise exemplary life.

Example: "The jury has found my elderly client guilty of negligence in this vehicular case. But in assessing any penalty, look at the complete picture of this distinguished gentleman's life. And I say to him, 'thanks for the memories.'"

■ victory gardens

Client/juror/witness age range: 69–84

Explanation: Backyard plots—sometimes just rows—of vegetables and fruits, grown voluntarily and without compensation by Americans in World War II to aid in the war effort by freeing farm produce for the armed forces.

Application: To establish character quality—volunteerism for the greater good, without compensation.

Example: "Far from ignoring the community, [my client] planted financial victory gardens—aid programs—there to help them win the war on poverty."

■ "The weed of crime bears bitter fruit"

Client/juror/witness age range: 69–84

Explanation: A tagline used in the 1940s popular anticrime drama radio series *The Shadow*.

Application: In addition to being a useful metaphor understood by people of all ages, it should stimulate memories among the Mature of radio dramas of years past when, as children, they were taught that criminal activity generates bad results.

Example: "The defendant's illegal activities have damaged and even destroyed the lives of numerous individuals. There is a saying that describes this now as well as it did criminal activity decades ago: 'The weed of crime bears bitter fruit.'"

■ "Whispering Hope"

Client/juror/witness age range: 69–84

Explanation: A 1940s song that speaks of brightness and hope after difficulty and sorrow.

Application: To show that the inspiring message of this song cannot apply to a dead crime victim.

Example: "Hope—for ourselves, for our children—it inspires us all. But it can't inspire the victim in this case, a young woman viciously raped and murdered by the defendant. I can't help thinking of the lovely and uplifting song 'Whispering Hope.' Maybe some of you remember it. It was recorded some years ago by Jo Stafford and Gordon MacRae. It speaks of sunshine and hope after darkness and tempest. But for this young woman, there is no sunshine, no hope, no happiness, no future. Only the darkness and rot of the grave, because of *this killer.*"

■ "You Always Hurt the One You Hate"

Client/juror/witness age range: 69–84

Explanation: A takeoff phrase based on the popular 1940s song "You Always Hurt the One You Love."

Application: To counter unexpressed prejudice against a client or witness by jurors of a different group—social, ethnic, class, or belief.

Example: "[My client] might be [for example, poor, black, Latino, or accused of a despicable crime—that is, in a category or categories that might arouse prejudice]. Some people might despise him just on that basis. They would turn around the old song 'You Always Hurt the One You Love' to 'You Always Hurt the One You Hate.' But I know that this jury does not harbor such prejudices. You will, I know, judge on the basis of the facts in evidence only."

■ "You'd Be So Nice to Come Home To"

Client/juror/witness age range: 69–84

Explanation: A World War II–era song about an anticipated marriage.

Application: To contrast the gentle, hopeful tone of the song with a killing that deprives someone of his or her sweetheart or fiancé(e).

Example: "They were going to be married. They were childhood sweethearts. But then she was run over and killed by this defendant, a drunk driver. There was a lovely song some years ago called 'You'd Be So Nice to Come Home To.' Perhaps some of you remember it. Well, [the fiancée's name] won't ever come home to him, because she's dead. All he can do now is visit her grave in the cemetery, because of *this drunk driver.*"

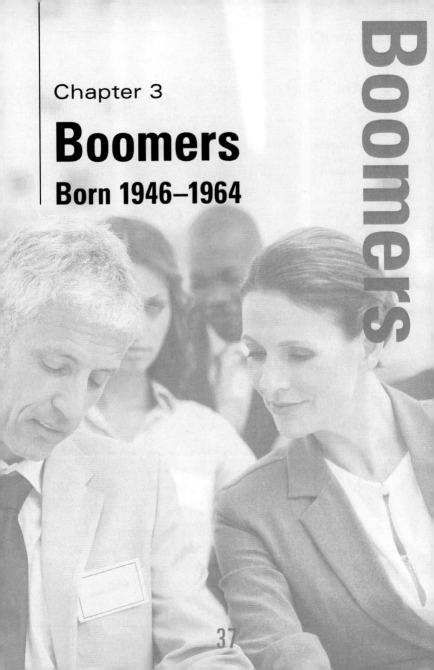

Chapter 3

Boomers
Born 1946–1964

Boomers

■ "Ain't That a Shame"

Client/juror/witness age range: 50–68

Explanation: A 1950s song about a romantic entanglement.

Application: To counter one's opponent's claim of lack of liability even though one has been harmed.

Example: "Respondent's counsel says his client bears no responsibility for my client's loss. It reminds me of the Fats Domino recording of the 1950s, 'Ain't That a Shame.' Because that in effect is what they're saying here. But we're not talking about one's love life. We submit that the respondent bears full responsibility for the harm he caused [my client]."

■ Darth Vader

Client/juror/witness age range: 50–68

Explanation: An evil character in the film *Star Wars*.

Application: Could be effective in generating memories among Boomers of a particularly vicious form of evil, if mentioned in the context of criticizing one's opponent's position.

Example: "This defendant—this drug lord—was merciless in murdering anyone who got in his way. He stomped out their lives as one might a bothersome insect. If you can imagine a modern-day version of Darth Vader, that is this vicious defendant."

■ "Everybody's Somebody's Fool"

Client/juror/witness age range: 50–68

Explanation: A song about taking advantage of emotional vulnerability in others.

Application: To prosecute an individual, group, or company that has used deceptive advertising to lure customers.

Example: "The defendants used deceptive ads to entice people to buy their products. They played with their emotions in a cynical ploy to make illegal profits. Back in the sixties, Connie Francis made a recording some of you might remember, 'Everybody's Somebody's Fool.' Maybe that's true, but the foolers don't have to get away with it. And in this case, I ask that you decide that they *won't* get away with it."

■ Graceland

Client/juror/witness age range: 50–68

Explanation: The home of Elvis Presley, which is now a very successful tourist attraction.

Application: To contrast this popular place, happy and nostalgic to Boomers, with a closed, secretive locale used for violent criminal purposes.

Example: "This 'residence' of the defendants—if such a name can be used to dignify it—was actually a trans-shipment dump for terrorist bombers. Not exactly Graceland—not exactly a place of warm memories of joyous years."

■ "The Great Pretender"

Client/juror/witness age range: 50–68

Explanation: A 1950s song about someone who pretends that his girlfriend has not left him.

Application: To reinforce that an individual's pretense deceived others and thus made him liable civilly or criminally.

Example: "His partners trusted him. Meanwhile, he was cooking the books to fleece them. Remember the Platters' song 'The Great Pretender'? That was this guy. But we're not talking about a lost love here. We're talking about the [amount] that he bilked from his partners."

■ Howdy Doody

Client/juror/witness age range: 50–68

Explanation: A child puppet character of "Buffalo Bob" Smith on a widely popular children's television program of the late 1940s and 1950s.

Application: Usable in asserting decreased liability for a spokesperson of an organization.

Example: "[My client's] substantive involvement in this matter is minimal. He appeared before the cameras, told the media what management's position was. But he did not make policy. To draw a comparison with what many of you remember from early TV, the voice was Howdy Doody's, but the ideas he spoke were Buffalo Bob's."

■ "I Can Dream, Can't I?"

Client/juror/witness age range: 50–68

Explanation: A plaintive song of the 1950s about a romantic fantasy.

Application: Usable to characterize one's opponent's weak case.

Example: "Opposing counsel's case is so weak it reminds me of a tune from the fifties by the Andrews Sisters—'I Can Dream, Can't I?' Because that seems to be their only hope, since the evidence, we submit, overwhelmingly supports [my client's] position."

■ "I Write the Songs"

Client/juror/witness age range: 50–68

Explanation: A 1970s single by Barry Manilow about songs that affect people.

Application: To draw a parallel between an influential songwriter and laws, which by definition are influential.

Example: "This defendant has blatantly and brazenly disregarded the law—clearly he is contemptuous of it. You know, some years ago Barry Manilow recorded a single, 'I Write the Songs'—about a songwriter whose compositions had an impact on people. Perhaps you remember it. Well, Mr. and Ms. Juror, 'We, the people' write the *laws*—and I ask that you find this defendant guilty for outrageously violating *our* laws."

John Wayne Gacy

Client/juror/witness age range: Principally 50–68, but his notoriety is pangenerational.

Explanation: A 1970s serial killer who secured the trust of adolescent boys, enticed them to work for him, and then murdered them.

Application: Could be used in an analogous fiscal sense to damn a "confidence man" swindler.

Example: "The defendant [or respondent] did not kill his victims physically. He was far more subtle than that. He gained their confidence, persuaded them to invest their money with him, and then bankrupted them by spending it for his own purposes. He's a financial John Wayne Gacy!"

■ "Look What They've Done to My Song"

Client/juror/witness age range: Remembered principally by those 50–68.

Explanation: A popular song of the early 1970s, it recounts the plaint of a songwriter whose song, "the only thing I've done half right," is "turning out all wrong" because of what others have done to it.

Application: To challenge the other party's handling of the case—twisting interpretation of the evidence, impugning your client's motives, etc.

Example: "Remember the seventies tune 'Look What They've Done to My Song'? Well, Mr. and Ms. Juror, let me rephrase that: Look what they've done to [my client]!"

■ "May the Truth be with you"

Client/juror/witness age range: 50–68

Explanation: A variation of a memorable line in the film *Star Wars*.

Application: Most Boomers were at an impressionable age when *Star Wars* was released. "May the Force be with you" was a strong, positive statement in that film. This trustful, encouraging variation could be effective if used in the context of a positive statement about one's client's case.

Example: "We have been open and honest about [defendant's first name]'s case, but now the verdict is in your hands. We ask you to weigh all the evidence carefully, and we trust in your good judgment. May the Truth be with you."

"My Way"

Client/juror/witness/age range: 50–68

Explanation: A late 1960s song popularized by Frank Sinatra.

Application: To establish that a unique lifestyle is not necessarily illegal.

Example: "My client is charged with a variety of minor offenses. Admittedly, his life is not mainstream: he wanders the streets at odd hours, he howls from time to time, he bellows loudly and at length at public meetings, he wears clothes that some might consider bizarre. Eccentric, yes; outlandish, yes; even bizarre; but not illegal. Back in the late sixties, Frank Sinatra popularized the song 'My Way,' about a man doing his own thing, charting his own course. We submit that a society that cracks down on any deviation is not a civilized society, and we urge that all charges be dropped."

■ "Strangers in the Night"

Client/juror/witness age range: 50–68

Explanation: A 1960s song about a couple who meet and develop a romantic relationship.

Application: To contrast this positive song with a nocturnal criminal attack.

Example: "The victim was out for an evening walk near his home. But then it turned ugly. Remember the 1960s Sinatra tune 'Strangers in the Night'? A nice song about a couple who meet, with positive results. But the strangers in this night were these defendants—vicious muggers who beat the victim senseless and then robbed him."

■ "Venus"

Client/juror/witness age range: Primarily Boomers (born 1946–1964), since the song reached its peak of popularity in 1970. However, it remained very popular through 1986, so it also would resonate with those in Generation X and Generation Y.

Explanation: A popular song of the 1970s and 1980s that told of beauty and love.

Application: To contrast the beautiful sentiments of the song, and of the Venus analogy in general, with a gross, repulsive crime.

Example: "You know, this crime makes me sick. I just want something clean and lovely to think about. Remember 'Venus,' by Shocking Blue? The song stayed popular in the seventies and eighties. It spoke of beauty and love. Venus was the Roman goddess of beauty and love. And Venus, the 'wishing star,' sparkles and shines in our evening sky. Contrast this loveliness with the ugly, brutish butchering of innocent victims by these defendants. Give them the kind of 'beauty' they deserve for their defilement—a prison cell!"

■ Watergate

Client/juror/witness age range: Although the Watergate scandal (1972–1974) occurred during Generation X's birth years (1965–1977), its major emotional impact was arguably on their immediately preceding generation, the Boomers, and thus is included among that group here.

Explanation: The most notorious American political scandal of the twentieth century, Watergate triggered the resignation of President Nixon and the resignation and conviction of his principal aides.

Application: To draw a parallel between the Watergate initial violation of law and subsequent aggravated cover-up, and a similar situation in business or government.

Example: "The situation for these corporate defendants went from bad to worse to worst. First, they illegally concealed losses in the company's annual report; then, in sworn testimony, they repeatedly covered up their deception. It is like a grim echo of the Watergate scandal of the seventies: a violation of the law that was aggravated by lies under oath, leading to disaster and disgrace."

■ "Your Cheatin' Heart"

Client/juror/witness age range: 50–68

Explanation: A song recorded by country singer Hank Williams; popular in the early 1950s and for decades thereafter, it talks about cheating in love.

Application: To attack the character of opposing counsel's client in financial or other matters.

Example: "Remember the old Hank Williams hit 'Your Cheatin' Heart'? Well, in this case, counselor, you can change it to 'your cheatin' client.'"

Chapter 4

Generation X
Born 1965–1977

■ "Alone"

Client/juror/witness age range: 37–49

Explanation: A song that talks of emotional isolation because of the absence of a loved one.

Application: To apply the song's expression of isolation to those deprived of a loved one because of a criminal act.

Example: "Kids are probably the most vulnerable members of our society. And they have needs—needs that only a mother can take care of. But the children of the victim in this case won't have those needs met by their mom—who had been their only living parent— because she's dead, murdered by this defendant. I keep thinking of Heart's song 'Alone,' about emotional isolation. Well, these kids are truly alone as far as their mother is concerned. Others may try to provide, but it's as if these children's hearts have been ripped out, because of *this killer.*"

■ the Berlin Wall

Client/juror/witness age range: 37–49

Explanation: The barrier erected in 1961 by East Germany in Berlin; the wall was leveled in 1989 with the collapse of communism in East Germany.

Application: To draw a parallel between the secrecy implied in the Berlin Wall and secrecy or extreme evasion in revealing, for example, required financial information.

Example: "If you have nothing to hide, why are you in effect stonewalling us about your financial records? You know, back in the eighties President Reagan, referring to the Berlin Wall, said to Mikhail Gorbachev, 'Tear down that wall!' Well, I say to you, 'Tear down that wall of secrecy about your records!'"

■ collapse of the Soviet Union

Client/juror/witness age range: Although this occurred in Generation Y's birth-year range (1978–1996), most of those in that generation were too young to understand the collapse fully, so it is included in this immediately previous age group.

Explanation: Following intense economic and political pressure, the government of the Soviet Union was dissolved in 1991, after seventy-four years of Communist dictatorship.

Application: To draw a parallel between the predatory Soviet Union and corporate criminal manipulators.

Example: "These defendants drove this company into the ground. They pillaged and plundered it for their gain and cheated their stockholders and employees to such an extent that the company is now a corporate basket case. It reminds me of the old Soviet Union, the 'evil empire' whose dictators exploited the people to enhance their own power. These rulers, like the notorious Joseph Stalin, were never made to answer in court for their crimes. But we live by the rule of law, and in this case, you can see to it that these defendants, rulers of their own corporate 'evil empire,' are brought to justice."

■ "Cuts Like a Knife"

Client/juror/witness age range: 37–49

Explanation: A 1983 rock song written by Bryan Adams and Jim Vallance.

Application: To contrast constructive pain with destructive pain.

Example: "There is good pain and there is bad pain. In the Bryan Adams/Jim Vallance song 'Cuts Like a Knife,' about the end of a relationship, the pain the person feels is actually cathartic—he emerges a better person. But in the case before us today, the defendant wielded a knife of a different sort—and with far different results. He stabbed and cut his victim dozens of times—and she is now in her grave. Send him to prison and let him know what the amputation of his freedom feels like."

■ "The Glamorous Life"

Client/juror/witness age range: 37–49

Explanation: A song that tells of living well.

Application: To contrast a lavish lifestyle with the illegal means used to achieve it.

Example: "They lived exceedingly well—high on the hog, as they say, with expensive homes and yachts. That's what these corporate managers did. And they did it, via a variety of illegal means that we will bring out, on the backs of their stockholders. You know, back in the eighties, Sheila E. recorded a song some of you might remember, 'The Glamorous Life.' Well, these defendants lived a very glamorous life, but now they must pay. Show them what kind of glamorous life there is in prison."

■ "I'll Be There for You"

Client/juror/witness age range: 37-49

Explanation: A song of personal commitment.

Application: Useful in personalizing one's position in jurors' minds during their deliberations.

Example: "We submit that the evidence shows that [the defendant's first name] should not have even been charged in this case. You know, some years ago Bon Jovi recorded a song some of you may remember—'I'll

Be There for You.' And that is what [the defendant's first name] asks of you in your deliberations. Please—be there for him in his innocence; return him to his loved ones."

▪ "It's My Life"

Client/juror/witness age range: 37–49

Explanation: A song that speaks of self-identity and self-awareness.

Application: For the defense: to emphasize that a life is at stake in a criminal case. For the prosecution: to emphasize that a life has been taken in a criminal case.

Example: "The fate of [the defendant's first name] is now in your hands. We submit that the evidence shows that he did not commit this crime. But remember, in a capital case such as this, a life is at stake. Perhaps you remember, some few years ago Talk Talk made a sensitive single called 'It's My Life.' And that's what [the defendant's first name] says to you today. Please return him where he belongs—to his [home, wife, children, etc.]."

If used by the prosecution, the opposite approach could be taken: "If he could speak from the grave, [the victim's first name] would say to this vicious murderer, 'It's my life you took.'"

■ "Runaway"

Client/juror/witness age range: 37–49

Explanation: A song about a girl who, ignored by her father when she lived at home, ran away to a life of urban prostitution.

Application: To elicit the compassion of the jury and/or court for a young person whose life has gone terribly wrong.

Example: "[The defendant's first name] is charged with prostitution and petty larceny. But there are other issues involved here. Back in the eighties, Bon Jovi made a song called 'Runaway'—perhaps some of you remember it. It makes me think of [defendant's first name]'s situation. She was thrown out of her house as a teenager and ran away to the city. Now she sells her body, and she also steals to support her drug addiction. We do not dispute the charges here. We ask for a suspended sentence on both counts and counseling and rehabilitation for this unfortunate girl."

■ "Self-Control"

Client/juror/witness age range: 37–49

Explanation: A song about loss of self-control.

Application: To appeal to jurors' higher instincts—in this case, their belief in their own self-control.

Example: "The defendant beat up his victim viciously and mercilessly. Why? Because of a domestic dispute. You know, back in the eighties Laura Branigan recorded a song called 'Self-Control'—about losing it. And that's what happened, only brutally in this case. In a civilized society, we can't just pummel someone because we are angry. We *must* exercise self-control. We ask that you find the defendant guilty as charged."

■ "Someone to Watch Over Me"

Client/juror/witness age range: This Gershwin song enjoyed revivals in later decades of the twentieth century and is included in this generation for that reason, but the song is recognizable back to those in Mature years.

Explanation: A song about being taken care of in a romantic/marriage relationship, it can be applied in more contemporary situations.

Application: To contrast the song's original protective intent with current invasive, invasion-of-privacy applications.

Example: "It's really outrageous what this defendant [identity stealer] has done to invade the privacy of and steal from my client. Remember the song 'Someone to Watch Over Me'? Linda Ronstadt and others recorded it. It tells of the wish for a benign, protective, loving relationship. Well, this defendant has corrupted that—he has 'watched over' my client without his permission, stealing his identity and substantial amounts of his money in the process."

▨ 2 + 2 = 5-ism

Client/juror/witness age range: 37–49

Explanation: Verbally "agreeing" with someone to end that person's constant hectoring. A false agreement, it could be considered the argumentative equivalent of a frolic and a banter.

Application: To invalidate a seeming agreement on the basis of verbal harassment.

Example: "Opposing counsel says my client agreed to buy [the other party's product]. To get rid of the constant badgering, he used the 2 + 2 = 5-ism approach: 'I'll agree with anything you say, just don't bother me anymore.' There was, in fact, *no* agreement."

▨ "When You Close Your Eyes"

Client/juror/witness age range: 37–49

Explanation: A song of self-reflection when one is about to go to sleep.

Application: Whether used by the defense or the prosecution, to tap into latent guilt feelings of jurors if they decide for the other side.

Example: "The verdict in this case is up to you. You are the judges of the facts, your decision will determine [the defendant's first name]'s future. And you must live with your decision. You know, back in the eighties, Night Ranger made a song called 'When You Close Your Eyes'—when you're about to fall asleep, thinking about what you've done. When you close your eyes after your deliberations, could you live with the fact that you condemned [the defendant's first name]? We hope that you will decide differently and find that the evidence shows that he is not guilty." If used by the prosecution: "Could you sleep peacefully knowing that you have released this vicious killer to prey on others?"

Chapter 5

Generation Y
Born 1978–1996

■ "All the Pain Money Can Buy"

Client/juror/witness age range: 18–36

Explanation: A CD that says that money can be used to make others suffer.

Application: To show that money can be used for evil ends—in this case, in a contract murder.

Example: "Terror can take many forms, and it need not be by foreign religious fanatics. In this case, it was bought—via hired killers, the defendants. They repeatedly threatened and attacked the victim until he went into hiding. But they tracked him down and murdered him. I'm reminded of Fastball's CD 'All the Pain Money Can Buy.' Here it bought pain, terror, and death. Please, find these pitiless thugs guilty and send them where they can no longer prey on civilized society."

■ beam up

Client/juror/witness age range: 18–36

Explanation: To get high on drugs.

Application: To establish the meaning of the term for those not familiar with it.

Example: "If you hear the term 'beam up' during this trial, it does not refer to space travel. It has a very serious, Earth-bound meaning. It means to get high on drugs."

■ blow the glass

Client/juror/witness age range: 18–36

Explanation: To smoke crack cocaine in a pipe.

Application: To establish the meaning of the term for those not familiar with it.

Example: "Be aware that the term 'blow the glass' might be used during this trial. It means to smoke crack cocaine in a pipe."

■ blunt; broccoli; dank; doobie

Client/juror/witness age range: 18–36

Explanation: All these terms mean marijuana.

Application: To establish the meaning of the terms for those not familiar with them.

Example: "You should know that the terms 'blunt,' 'broccoli,' 'dank,' and 'doobie' might be used during this trial. They all mean marijuana."

■ "A Change Would Do You Good"

Client/juror/witness age range: 18–36

Explanation: A song that advises a change from a dysfunctional life.

Application: To show that even being sent to prison would benefit someone living in a criminal environment.

Example: "The young defendant in this case has been found guilty of petty larceny previously, but now he is before this court on a charge of armed robbery. I submit that the evidence will show him guilty of this crime, and I also submit that he serve prison time, to reform him. He has spent his entire life in a section of this city that generates crime—that's all he knows. I'm reminded of Sheryl Crow's song 'A Change Would Do You Good.' Well, a change would do this young man good, even if it be in prison, for it would show him that there are things in life other than crime."

■ "Dangerous"

Client/juror/witness age range: 18–36

Explanation: A song that says to be careful of predators in emotional relationships.

Application: To illustrate that caution is needed with strangers, particularly children and those who would prey on them.

Example: "This defendant picked his victim carefully, in a pattern that is sickeningly familiar—a lone boy on a playground, isolated from the other children. The offer of candy, or maybe of seeing newborn kittens; the isolation; and then the attack. I keep thinking of the song

'Dangerous' by Roxette, about being very careful about whom to trust. This child is already a victim, and this defendant must pay for his crime, but we must impress on our children the danger that he and his kind pose to them."

■ flash mob

Client/juror/witness age range: 18–36

Explanation: An often impromptu and frequently violent crowd usually focused on an issue.

Application: To establish this crowd as the cause of a client's injury or death.

Example: "My client was simply in the wrong place at the wrong time. She was trampled by a flash mob, an impromptu protest crowd surging through her neighborhood. She had nothing to do with it."

■ footchild

Client/juror/witness age range: 18–36

Explanation: In a custody situation, a child who is shuttled between mother and father; in a football analogy, much like a football (*foot*ball + *child*).

Application: To confirm that the child's interests are paramount, not the parents', in any custody arrangement.

Example: "It's like the mother and father are playing a game here. He gets so much time with their child, she gets so much time. It's like a game of football, with the child the ball. He [or she] has become a 'footchild'— football plus child. But he [or she] is a young, vulnerable person, not an object to be kicked back and forth."

■ "Free Your Mind"

Client/juror/witness age range: 18–36

Explanation: A song that asks the listener to avoid stereotypes when evaluating people.

Application: To counter "profiling" or other stereotypical behavior in judging the culpability of someone accused of a crime.

Example: "There were bombs found in my client's apartment building. And he has been accused of putting them there, with no evidence, I submit, to support that contention. But he is young, and an Arab, and Muslim. Does that make him guilty? Back in the nineties, En Vogue recorded a single called 'Free Your Mind.' It earnestly asks us to avoid stereotyping or 'profiling' when judging others. And so I ask you in this case. My client's age, ethnicity, and religion do not make him guilty. And neither does the evidence."

■ "The Hardest Thing"

Client/juror/witness age range: 18–36

Explanation: A song that describes the difficulty of doing something painful.

Application: In asking, for example, a jury to overcome any sympathy toward a defendant based on emotion and to decide solely on the facts in evidence in the case.

Example: I know—you know—that this teenager on trial seems the picture of innocence; he's clean-cut, neatly dressed, and has had an excellent record in school. All positives. He just seems *likable*. Well, back in the nineties, 98 Degrees made a record you might remember, 'The Hardest Thing.' And now I'm asking you to do what might be the hardest thing for you. *On the overwhelming basis of the evidence*, this defendant fatally stabbed a classmate repeatedly. So please put aside whatever personal sympathy you might have for this killer and find him guilty of [murder/manslaughter].

■ hutenance

Client/juror/witness age range: 18–36

Explanation: Minimal maintenance of humans (human + maintenance)—a situation wherein institutions such as nursing homes, prisons, and orphanages literally warehouse those in their care.

Application: To point out deficiencies in institutional care, such as nursing homes where the elderly are just left to grow older from day to day, prisons without meaningful rehabilitation programs, and orphanages with little variety for the children.

Example: "The program at the [nursing home name] needs to be overhauled. The elderly there get just the minimum to keep them alive. Otherwise, they're left to just get older, like items in a warehouse. There's a word that describes their condition: hutenance—that's human plus maintenance. People—certainly those in their so-called golden years—deserve better."

■ schizonomics

Client/juror/witness age range: 18–36

Explanation: An economic "analysis" offered in a civil case that is so distorted and twisted that it seems separated from reality.

Application: To help counter an opponent's complicated economic explanation by reducing it to a word that suggests it can't be understood.

Example: "I don't know about you, but the plaintiff's [or respondent's] economic so-called analysis in this case leaves me going around in circles. You know, the word root 'schizo' implies a separation from reality. I think that the plaintiff [or respondent] has in effect coined a new word here: 'schizonomics.' Because that is what their gibberish adds up to."

■ the "Unabomber"

Client/juror/witness age range: 18–36

Explanation: Theodore John Kaczynski was a reclusive genius and self-styled crusader against modern technology who, between 1978 and 1995, mailed homemade bombs to try to make his political points, killing three and wounding twenty-three. In 1998 he was sentenced to life in prison without parole.

Application: To show that high intelligence and an at least arguable point of view do not justify murder in a civilized society.

Example: "The defendant and his victim in this case were mortal political enemies. The defendant termed him a lethal threat to us all. We will show that the defendant was in fact the lethal one and that he had his opponent assassinated in a contract killing. Remember Ted Kaczynski, the 'Unabomber'? He tried to make his political points by murder and is now serving a life sentence without parole. The defendant here is in fact a later version of Kaczynski. If it is acceptable to prevail politically by murder, then civilization collapses. Give the defendant the same fate as the Unabomber."

Chapter 6

Pangenerational

Alzheimer's

Client/juror/witness age range: All ages

Explanation: A progressively degenerative brain disease that ultimately results in death.

Application: To draw a parallel between the degeneration of Alzheimer's and the progressive breakdown of a business by illegal means.

Example: "The defendants in this case are specialists—they specialize in corporate death. After they bought [name the company], they set to their terminal task. Like the degenerative cells of Alzheimer's disease, they systematically, and illegally, milked the company of its assets and its good name for their own profit, so that today it is a wrecked and useless corporate hulk."

as stable as a teeter-totter

Client/juror/witness age range: All ages

Explanation: An antithetical statement.

Application: To ridicule one's opponent's case by comparing it to the inherent instability of a teeter-totter.

Example: "Opposing counsel's 'case' is based on witnesses arguably not there, flimsy 'facts,' and conclusions based on this mishmash. And then he insults your intelligence by asking you to believe him. In fact, his 'case' is as stable as a teeter-totter."

■ "bad" for "formidable"

Client/juror/witness age range: All ages

Explanation: In black English, "bad" has a meaning of "formidable" or "very effective." The term "badass" is also sometimes used.

Application: To educate jurors not familiar with black English of this usage, to avoid misunderstanding.

Example: "Let me emphasize this: When [my client] calls someone 'bad' or a 'badass,' he means someone who is formidable or very effective, not evil."

■ "beautiful wickedness"

Client/juror/witness age range: All ages

Explanation: In *The Wizard of Oz*, a self-reference by the Wicked Witch of the West as she melted.

Application: To demonstrate that something can be simultaneously beautiful and evil.

Example: "The defendant here promoted herself as a collector of fine art. Or so it seemed. In reality, she expertly forged numerous copies of fine artwork and

71

sold them as originals to unsuspecting collectors. You might remember, in *The Wizard of Oz*, the Wicked Witch of the West referred to her "beautiful wickedness" as she melted. I want you to keep that phase in mind as you examine the evidence and hear the testimony of the expert witnesses in this case. For the copies are truly beautiful, but their sale was unquestionably wicked."

■ Benedict Arnold

Client/juror/witness age range: All ages

Explanation: An American general in the Revolutionary War, he secretly passed important information to the British and defected to their side. His name has become synonymous with betrayal.

Application: To draw a parallel between the notorious traitor Benedict Arnold and a modern-day betrayer of trust.

Example: "The defendant [or respondent] was considered to be a very talented, if temperamental, employee of [name the company]. But he believed that he did not receive the credit he deserved and that he was unfairly bypassed for promotion. He had been entrusted with vital, proprietary information by his company, but he betrayed that trust by secretly revealing that information to the company's principal competitor. He is nothing less than a modern-day corporate Benedict Arnold, the infamous traitor of the Revolutionary War!"

■ brainwashing

Client/juror/witness age range: All ages

Explanation: Coercive or forcible indoctrination to persuade someone to change some or all of his basic positions or beliefs.

Application: To mitigate guilt for an illegal act after one has been brainwashed to perform the act.

Example: "My client is a naive eighteen-year-old with no prior record of violence. His so-called friends persuaded him to join their cult, which maintains that devils from hell have overrun the world. The cult harried, harassed, and hectored him until he internalized their beliefs. Then they threatened him. They told him if he did not kill the devils' leader, Satan—in reality, a reporter investigating the cult—that he, himself, would be cast into hell for all eternity. They wanted him to do their dirty work for them. Panicked, my client did as he was ordered—he killed the reporter. He admits it. What I submit we have here, ladies and gentlemen, is a gross example of brainwashing of my client, a very suggestible young man. Please keep that in mind as you assess guilt in this case."

■ cancer

Client/juror/witness age range: All ages

Explanation: A self-destructive disease that often, if not usually, develops as a result of cellular abuse.

Application: To draw a parallel between cellular abuse resulting in cancer and personal abuse resulting in what could be called behavioral cancers.

Example: "[The defendant's first name] was beaten by her parents, and they withheld any kind of love from her. She finally ran away as a teenager and took up with an older man, who offered her love—but on his own destructive terms. Like a healthy cell that had become cancerous, she turned into a bitter, antisocial creature. We do not contest the charge against her, but in light of her traumatic background, ask for a suspended sentence, counseling, and rehabilitation."

▪ cook the books

Client/juror/witness age range: All ages

Explanation: Falsification of financial statements.

Application: To compare culinary cooking with financial cooking.

Example: "Let me draw a food analogy about what this defendant did. When you cook food, that's good—it's often necessary, to eliminate harmful bacteria. But this defendant, the chief financial officer of his company, cooked something else—the books. When someone cooks the books, he makes fraudulent, dishonest financial entries. Send this defendant to prison for illegally ruining the stockholders' money meal!"

■ death

Client/juror/witness age range: All ages

Explanation: The final end of anything, be it life, a situation, or a business.

Application: To have jurors draw a parallel between the trauma of a personal death and the financial trauma of a corporate death.

Example: "The defendants here—top management—were responsible for nurturing their company, keeping it alive and healthy. But like quack doctors, they allowed it to become sick and finally terminal. And the employees and stockholders are the losers. We urge that these defendants be found negligent in allowing the company to die."

■ demolition derby

Client/juror/witness age range: All ages

Explanation: A contest in which cars—or humans—collide to determine the last functional survivor.

Application: To show that there can be exceptions to what is otherwise widespread chaotic activity.

Example: "My client does not belong to a gang. But when all-out war erupted among the gangs in his neighborhood—it was like a demolition derby—he was caught in the middle. He had nothing to do with the mayhem—he was simply walking to his home—but when the police came to arrest the participants, [give the client's first name] was arrested along with the others *because he looked like them*—racial profiling carried to a gross extreme. I submit that all charges should be dropped against my client because there is not one shred of evidence that he had anything to do with this violence."

■ double negative for single negative

Client/juror/witness age range: All ages

Explanation: Use of two negatives—technically a positive—when a single negative is meant. Not exclusive to any one race, ethnic group, or generation, but typically associated with those with limited formal education. "I didn't do nothin'" means "I didn't do anything."

Application: To enter into the record with the transcript and to instruct the jury about this idiomatic construction so that statements by one's clients or witnesses are not misconstrued.

Example: "Please understand that when [one's client or witness] says things such as 'I didn't do nothin',' he means he didn't do *any*thing. A simple negative is what he means."

■ earthquake

Client/juror/witness age range: All ages

Explanation: A shaking, trembling, or upheaval of the earth.

Application: The term can be applied to a variety of situations, such as the economic example below.

Example: "This plant had become a cornerstone of the community. It had employed generations of the town's residents. So when the parent company summarily shut the plant down, it decimated the town as surely as if an earthquake had hit it—throwing hundreds out of work and making the town an economically unstable place."

■ emotional bullets

Client/juror/witness age range: All ages

Explanation: Harassment, taunting, or other emotional pressure that can be as destructive psychologically as bullets can be physically.

Application: To establish mitigating circumstances when one has responded physically to emotional attacks.

Example: "[First name of the defendant] was taunted unmercifully at school by a pack of students. They demeaned him, attacked his self-esteem, made him feel like trash. Then something snapped. He took his father's gun and shot to death the worst harasser. We don't deny that he did it, but we do say that there were clear mitigating circumstances. He himself had been shot repeatedly—not with steel, but with numerous emotional bullets, which savagely lodged in his psyche until he broke."

F. W. de Klerk and Nelson Mandela

Client/juror/witness age range: All ages

Explanation: Frederik Willem de Klerk was president of South Africa from 1989 to 1994. Nelson Rolihlahla Mandela succeeded him in that office until 1999. They shared the 1993 Nobel Peace Prize.

Application: To show that individuals and groups with vastly different views can negotiate a peaceful compromise.

Example: "The parties in this negotiation process couldn't be farther apart. Not only do they hold widely divergent positions, but they also dislike each other personally. Hopeless? Not necessarily. Let me give you an example. In 1993, the South Africans F. W. de Klerk and Nelson Mandela shared the 1993 Nobel Peace Prize. Why? Despite coming from vastly different cultures and their interpersonal animosity, they worked out a peaceful transition from apartheid-era South Africa to a fully democratic one. The parties in the dispute before us can, and should, follow their example."

geodump

Client/juror/witness age range: All ages

Explanation: Planet Earth as a dump (*geo*, Earth, + *dump*).

Application: To extend, in a jury's mind, the consequences of a defendant's pollution if it were worldwide.

Example: "This company has an abysmal record of systematically polluting the areas, including the waterways, near its factories. It's time it was brought to heel once and for all. Think what would happen if everyone had a culture of garbage the way this company has. The world would be a geodump—that's *geo*, for our Earth, and *dump*, for what this company is doing to the environment."

"Give him a decision he can't refuse"

Client/juror/witness age range: All ages

Explanation: A variation of arguably the most memorable quote from *The Godfather*.

Application: To contrast the coercive message of the quote in the film—agree or suffer terrible consequences—with an appeal to a jury for justice.

Example: "All [the client's first name] asks for here is justice. You know, in *The Godfather* Don Vito Corleone says, 'I'm gonna make him an offer he can't refuse.' But that was negative—intimidating, a threat. Now I ask that you give [the client's first name] something positive. Give him a *decision* he can't refuse. Find this good man not guilty and return him home to his wife and children."

■ Gordian knot

Client/juror/witness age range: All ages

Explanation: In Greek mythology, a difficult problem that was solved by a single, bold act.

Application: To petition a court to use its power to supersede an administrative rule.

Example: "My client is incarcerated in the state penitentiary. His elderly mother is dying of cancer and only wants to see her son before she dies. But the prison has a regulation forbidding a convict from leaving for such a visit. His mother has only days to live. I ask the court to cut this Gordian knot and allow my client to visit, if not for himself, then for his dying mother."

■ Hobson's choice

Client/juror/witness age range: All ages

Explanation: An apparently free choice when there is no realistic alternative.

Application: To establish coercion or at least mitigating circumstances when one is involved in an illegal activity.

Example: "You know, [first name of the defendant] is a good kid. He studies hard in school, he works after school, and he's never been on drugs. He wants to become a doctor. But he lives in a tough neighborhood. In this case, the gang in control there told him he had to stand watch over the people in a store while the gang robbed the store. They said if he didn't do it, they would kill him and his sister. So he did what they said. But during the robbery, a store employee was killed, and now [first name of the defendant] is charged in a felony murder. But he was caught in a Hobson's choice—he had no real alternative than to do as they said. They had a gun to his head. I ask that the charge against him be dismissed."

■ homicidal blackmail

Client/juror/witness age range: All ages

Explanation: Blackmail in which the "price" is the killing of a third party.

Application: To diminish guilt in which the perpetrator has been blackmailed into committing an illegal act.

Example: "My client is a single father. He and his only child, a seven-year-old daughter, were taking a walk together when his daughter was suddenly and violently snatched away from him and disappeared into a crowd. He received a note from the kidnappers—who, we have since found, are a gang of sadistic cutthroats—saying that unless he killed one of their enemies and did not inform the police, he would never see his daughter alive. Desperate, he did as he was told, in what amounts to homicidal blackmail. His daughter was returned to him alive—thrown in a ditch, raped, and grossly and permanently disfigured. Now he is in jail, on a charge of murder. It's enough to make you weep. [Pause.] I implore you to keep the plight of this poor man and his daughter in mind as you determine any guilt in this case."

■ Jackie Robinson

Client/juror/witness age range: All ages

Explanation: The first African American to break the color barrier in modern major league baseball; as such, a symbol of courage.

Application: To establish the character of someone accused or found guilty in a legal action, or of a witness.

Example: "Not only did my client not steal the money in question, he also, like Jackie Robinson, had the character—the guts, if you will—to endure slights and even slurs as the first African American member of his fraternity."

■ "Just when I thought I was out, they pull me back in"

Client/juror/witness age range: All ages

Explanation: External pressure as expressed by Michael Corleone in *Godfather 3*.

Application: To show that guilt can be mitigated or even absolved because of coercion.

Example: "My client left the [name the criminal gang] two years ago. He decided to live a clean life and was studying to become a teacher. But the gang had other ideas. They told him he had to return and drive their getaway car. You might remember in *Godfather 3* Michael Corleone said, 'Just when I thought I was out, they pull me back in.' But this gang did more than pull. They put a gun to [give the client's first name]'s head and told him they would kill him and his family unless he did as they told him. [Give the client's first name] obliged. Now he is charged as an accomplice in a felony. I submit that because my client was subject to aggravated coercion, this charge against him should be dropped."

■ "lead us not into temptation"

Client/juror/witness age range: All ages

Explanation: An injunction from the Lord's Prayer.

Application: To demonstrate the contrast between this injunction and its violation.

Example: "You know, the Lord's Prayer says, 'lead us not into temptation.' Instead, in this case, these so-called parents cursed their very young children with the opposite. The children are malnourished, live in filthy conditions, and, worse yet, have been corrupted by these people. The father, in drunken stupors, gave his seven-year-old son hard liquor to drink. Now, three years later, the boy is an alcoholic. The mother, constantly high, left drugs loose around the apartment. Her daughter, age eight, is now a drug addict. Our legal system won't permit it, but these parents should be horsewhipped. Instead, take these pitiful children away from these creatures permanently and prosecute these abusers to the full extent of the law."

■ Mickey Mouse

Client/juror/witness age range: All ages

Explanation: A Disney cartoon character created in 1928 and still popular today, it means insignificant or trivial.

Application: To use a universally recognized icon to make a point.

Example: "The defendants in this case bilked their investors of many millions of dollars. This was no Mickey Mouse operation."

■ one "swell foop"

Client/juror/witness age range: All ages

Explanation: Switching of initial letters in a phrase to make a point opposite to the original.

Application: Usable to mock opposing counsel's arguments using a single, transposed phrase—one "swell foop" for one "fell swoop."

Example: "Opposing counsel asks you to believe that the weight of evidence is on his side, that his is an open-and-shut case. But we submit that his case is littered with inconsistencies, that his witnesses' reliability is suspect, that in reality his case is in tatters. We say that, far from winning in one 'fell swoop,' his case collapses in one 'swell foop.'"

■ police kidnapping

Client/juror/witness age range: All ages

Explanation: An arrest that is itself a crime.

Application: To establish that those in law enforcement can be guilty of crime themselves.

Example: "My client has recently begun to investigate police corruption in this city {town, etc.], and the police are well aware of his activities in this area. Now they have arrested him on spurious charges to, I submit, tarnish his reputation and to deflect attention from their own malfeasance. I further submit that this 'arrest' is in fact a police kidnapping, that these accusers wearing the police uniform and badge are rogue cops, violators of the public trust, and that they should not be applying handcuffs but wearing them."

Psycho shower scene

Client/juror/witness age range: All ages

Explanation: The scene in this 1960 movie in which Norman Bates, dressed as his mother, stabs Marion Crane to death.

Application: To draw a parallel between this film killing and a similar homicide in real life.

Example: "No murder makes sense, but this one staggers the mind. The defendant leaped, seemingly out of nowhere, at the victim and repeatedly stabbed her to death. He didn't even take any money; he just ran off. Remember the shower scene in Hitchcock's *Psycho*, where the deranged motel owner stabs the woman to death? It's a chilling and apt parallel. But this is real life, and the killer must pay for his senseless act."

■ public trough

Client/juror/witness age range: All ages

Explanation: Government assistance and subsidies viewed as, in effect, a bottomless pit to be looted.

Application: To establish that to receive government support fraudulently is illegal.

Example: "The organization on trial before us received government support for its programs. Nothing wrong with that in principle, but the people running this organization weren't thinking in terms of principle—more in terms of their own bank accounts: they submitted bloated statements of their so-called costs, for projects that never took place, for jobs that never existed. Government subsidies became for them a public trough, to be plundered voraciously."

■ rats and roaches

Client/juror/witness age range: All ages

Explanation: Filthy creatures that typically inhabit urban areas.

Application: To compare hidden, repulsive practices with urban vermin.

Example: "On trial before you is a public official who used the cover of his office to conceal coercion, bribe-taking, and payoffs from drug dealers. He is no better than the rats and roaches that infest the sewers and alleyways whose maintenance he ignored. Flush this public vermin down the municipal toilet."

■ "Round up the usual suspects"

Client/juror/witness age range: All ages

Explanation: Arguably the most memorable line from the classic 1942 film *Casablanca.*

Application: To establish that although one may have had nothing to do with a particular crime, he still can be caught up in a police dragnet.

Example: "My client, [first name of the defendant], was having a few drinks with his buddies in a bar. He knew that some of the people there did drugs, but he didn't— not since leaving prison after his one conviction for marijuana possession. He was off parole but was known to the police. Well, that night the police raided the bar and arrested [first name of the defendant] for drug *dealing*, on their sole contention that some of his friends were dealing drugs. I'm reminded of the classic line by Captain Renault in *Casablanca*, 'Round up the usual suspects.' Well, being a 'usual suspect' doesn't mean you did the act, any more than it did in that film. I submit that the charge against my client be dismissed for lack of credible evidence."

■ salad days

Client/juror/witness age range: All ages

Explanation: One's flourishing period or heyday.

Application: To contrast an earlier, prosperous period with one of hardship.

Example: "My client [give first name]—whom I am representing pro bono—is the embodiment of what a loving husband and father should be. He and his wife have cared for their son with Down's syndrome since birth. [Give the client's first name] is now elderly, and his wife has terminal cancer; her care has drained all their savings. In my client's salad days, when he was much younger and working, he could have handled these problems. But now he can barely afford a salad to eat. And the bank has initiated foreclosure proceedings on their modest home. I ask for a stay on this foreclosure until some financial arrangement can be worked out to keep this burdened family from being thrown into the street."

■ scapegoat

Client/juror/witness age range: All ages

Explanation: Someone who is blamed for an act or acts he did not commit.

Application: To show that planted "evidence" can be a major problem for the plantee.

Example: "My client's car was parked on [name the street] in this city [or town]. Unfortunately, he had not locked the car. A gang of drug dealers, having held up a supplier down the block and then murdered him, raced down the street, opened the door of the first unlocked car they found—my client's—and threw the murder weapon in as well as a stash of crack cocaine. My client is now on trial for felony murder as well as for drug possession. I submit to you, ladies and gentlemen, that this innocent man is just a scapegoat, that he had nothing to do with these illegal activities."

■ shame

Client/juror/witness age range: All ages

Explanation: Deeply felt guilt.

Application: To highlight public responsibility to those who have labored for the public.

Example: "I rise to condemn the proposal at this proceeding to severely cut the pensions of former employees of this city [state, town, etc.], many of whom are absolutely dependent on them, to try to address a financial shortfall. Unfortunately such an unjust policy is not new. In 1890, in his poem 'The Last of the Light Brigade,' Rudyard Kipling eloquently gave voice to the plight of veterans of the Light Brigade, whose charge in the Crimean War thirty-six years earlier had been celebrated in Alfred, Lord Tennyson's poem 'The Charge of the Light Brigade.' Many of the veterans of that brigade were penniless or starving, but the English paid them virtually no pension. Kipling looked to the day when 'the fatted souls of the English were scourged with the thing called shame.' Today, this city should be greater than to have to scourge its soul with shame. Restore the pensions of those who have worked so long for them."

■ "Shoot first and ask questions later"

Client/juror/witness age range: All ages

Explanation: Instruction by Nazi high official Hermann Goering to the Prussian police in 1933.

Application: To make a connection between a policy of the Nazi police state and the act, sanctioned by his superiors, of a trigger-happy police officer today.

Example: "The police officer on trial here, after stopping the victim's car, asked him to produce his driver's license and car registration. When he reached toward the glove compartment to comply, the officer shot him in the arm five times, shattering it irreparably, so that today he has a prosthesis instead of an arm. The officer said he thought the driver was reaching for a gun. What's more, the officer's superiors said his act was justified. You know, some years ago, when the Nazis came to power, the notorious Hermann Goering instructed the Prussian police, 'Shoot first and ask questions later, and if you make mistakes, I will protect you.' Mr. and Ms.

Juror, police arrogance with firearms didn't die with the Nazis. It festers even today. I ask that you find this police officer guilty of [the appropriate charge]."

■ Sisyphean burden

Client/juror/witness age range: All ages

Explanation: In Greek mythology, King Sisyphus of Corinth was condemned eternally in Hades to roll a heavy rock up a steep hill, only to have it roll down again as it nears the top.

Application: To establish that one should not be penalized for being put, in effect, in a no-win situation.

Example: "My client faced an impossible task. As chief financial officer of the company, he was tasked with investing and spending the company's funds wisely. But when he became CFO, the company had a crushing debt burden. His financial strategies were wise; he made money for the company, but the debt interest wiped it out. I'm reminded of the story in Greek mythology of King Sisyphus, who was condemned eternally in Hades to roll a heavy rock up a steep hill, but then it would roll down again as it neared the top. My client truly had a Sisyphean burden. But the board of directors, looking for a scapegoat, fired him for not making a net profit, and now they want to illegally deprive him of benefits to which he is entitled."

■ spoiled brat

Client/juror/witness age range: All ages

Explanation: A characterization for an overindulged teenager or young adult.

Application: To show that one is subject to the law despite wealth.

Example: "He has had all the advantages—rich family, expensive prep schools, vacations at European resorts. He was denied nothing, but with privilege came arrogance—he became a headstrong, spoiled brat. And he became involved in alcohol and drug use. When he got into a drunken, drug-addled rage and wrecked a bar or club, he knew that his father would pay for it. But now he is in real trouble—during his latest tirade, he spat in the face of the investigating officer. He can't buy his way out of that. Perhaps the penitentiary will straighten him out. There he will clean toilets instead of sailing on Daddy's yacht and will eat prison food instead of the *quail en caisses à la Lamballe* he is used to."

■ stinking armpit

Client/juror/witness age range: All ages

Explanation: A repulsive human condition.

Application: Using an unpleasant term to counter a pleasant appearance.

Example: "The person being judged today is of a lower order of humanity. The buildings he owns and rents out are dilapidated; the maintenance, virtually nonexistent; he has violated numerous housing codes. And don't be fooled by this slumlord's dapper appearance—he's the stinking armpit of urban housing. Instead of the fragrance of the cologne he applies to himself, think of the stench of the raw sewage overflowing from the toilets that don't work in his buildings. Bring down the full force of the law on this creature."

■ terrorize; terrorism

Client/juror/witness age range: All ages

Explanation: One of the most potent terms in contemporary English; to terrorize need not be confined to physical violence.

Application: The term also means "to fill with anxiety" or "to scare," and it can apply to a variety of situations, such as in the financial example below.

Example: "The defendant lied to his elderly victims that he would seize their assets unless they paid him huge 'service charges' on their loans. It was nothing less than financial terrorism."

■ "There's a sucker born every minute"

Client/juror/witness age range: All ages

Explanation: A statement attributed to circus impresario P. T. Barnum.

Application: To reinforce that con artists are still around.

Example: "The defendant knowingly imported toys that he knew could be dangerous. But he promoted them as safe, and many parents believed him. Now a child has choked to death from a loose part on one of his toys. You know, back in the nineteenth century, circus showman P. T. Barnum is supposed to have said, 'There's a sucker born every minute.' Perhaps 'sucker' is the right word for the parents of this dead child. And perhaps 'murderer' [or other term, as appropriate] is the right word for this defendant."

■ the *Titanic*

Client/juror/witness age range: All ages

Explanation: The ocean liner that sank on its maiden voyage in April 1912 when it hit an iceberg in the North Atlantic, with the loss of 1,503 lives.

Application: To parallel the preventable *Titanic* tragedy with a preventable contemporary tragedy.

Example: "The fire disaster in this nightclub never should have happened. It could have been prevented. I can't help thinking of the *Titanic* tragedy, which also was preventable. There, they were going far too fast in those treacherous waters. Here, the sprinkler system was not up to code. There, there were too many people for the available lifeboats, with the loss of more than fifteen hundred lives. Here, the number of people in the club far exceeded the legal capacity, with panic, tramplings, jammed exits, and the loss of [state the number] lives."

■ tornado

Client/juror/witness age range: All ages

Explanation: A destructive, whirling wind with a funnel-shaped cloud.

Application: The term can be applied to a variety of situations, such as in the following example.

Example: "The rioters' destruction seemingly knew no bounds. Like a vicious tornado, the mob evidently moved at random through the community, bypassing some blocks and then ravaging the next."

■ unpopular war

Client/juror/witness age range: All ages

Explanation: A war that is unpopular with a significant number of the people in the country initiating the war.

Application: To draw a parallel between unpopular political policies and unpopular corporate policies.

Example: "This proxy vote is in effect a vote on the policies of top management, which have come under increasing criticism by the stockholders. It is much like a referendum on an unpopular war—not enough to indict a president or his top advisers, but enough to call for a change in leadership."

■ wastrel

Client/juror/witness age range: All ages

Explanation: An irresponsible, often young, reckless, and self-indulgent handler of money or other resources.

Application: To show that bad judgment in assigning financial responsibilities can lead to fiscal disaster.

Example: "The son of the president of the victimized company in this case was the apple of his father's eye, such that he made him special assistant to the company's chief financial officer. Unfortunately, Junior—the defendant before us—saw it as an opportunity to blow the company's money on gambling, women, and expensive cars. Since Daddy didn't teach this wastrel to be law-abiding, I submit that you send him to a place that will—prison."

"What would you have done?"

Client/juror/witness age range: All ages

Explanation: A question to encourage jurors to identify with the accused.

Application: To establish extreme stress to justify a violent act.

Example: "The man involved in this case broke into the house of my client, a single mom, and held her and her infant daughter prisoners at knifepoint. When she refused his demand that she be tied up and taken, with the infant, to an unknown destination, he cut off one of the infant's fingers and said he would go after the little girl's eyes next. As chance—or perhaps fate—would have it, my client was standing near her fireplace, grabbed a poker, and delivered one blow with it to his head to disable him, rendering him unconscious. She called the police, but the man later died from the blow. Now they have accused her of murder. And now I put it to you: What would you have done?"

■ *The Wizard of Oz* and lawyers

Client/juror/witness age range: All ages

Explanation: A takeoff of a statement by the Wizard in the film (see the Example section below).

Application: To vary a well-known line from a classic film to attack opposing counsel's case.

Example: "You know, in *The Wizard of Oz*, the Wizard says, 'I'm a very good man. I'm just a very bad wizard.' Well, I say, opposing counsel is a very good lawyer. He just has a very bad case."

■ yesterday's dishwater

Client/juror/witness age range: All ages

Explanation: A bland, unattractive substance that could be used in a critical analogy.

Application: To emphasize the weakness of one's opponent's case.

Example: "First, let me say that opposing counsel is a nice, pleasant guy. But he also has a weak, tepid, flat case. The law isn't on his side; neither are the facts. When you come down to it, his case compares to yesterday's dishwater."

■ "You can't fool any of this jury any of the time"

Client/juror/witness age range: All ages

Explanation: A variation of a quote by Lincoln to a caller at the White House, in Alexander K. McClure's *Lincoln's Yarns and Stories* (1904).

Application: To adapt a Lincoln quote to establish in the jury's mind that they can't be fooled by opposing counsel's arguments.

Example: "Opposing counsel has tried to stretch some fractured arguments to make a case for his side, but it all falls apart like a cheap suit. You know, Lincoln once said, 'You can't fool all of the people all of the time.' And I say about opposing counsel's case, 'You can't fool any of this jury any of the time.'"

Chapter 7

Literary

■ "All the world's a stage"

Client/juror/witness age range: All ages

Explanation: A phrase from Shakespeare's *As You Like It*, Act II.

Application: To establish that although life can resemble a theater drama, we are in control of the outcome.

Example: "You have seen and heard all the evidence in this case, and Judge [give the last name] will instruct you as to the law. We believe that the evidence shows that [give your client's first and last name] is not guilty. I can't impress on you enough the importance of your decision—a life is at stake here. You know, Shakespeare said, 'All the world's a stage, and all the men and women merely players.' That was a line in a play, but this is real life. Please—don't make this real-life drama a tragedy for [give your client's first name only]. Find him not guilty."

■ "as make the angels weep"

Client/juror/witness age range: All ages

Explanation: A phase from Shakespeare's *Measure for Measure*, Act II.

Application: To extend the nature of a crime beyond the earthly, to a religious level.

102

Example: "The crime here is unspeakably outrageous. A small, innocent child was raped and then viciously butchered. Shakespeare said that man was sometimes so arrogant 'as make the angels weep.' Ladies and gentlemen, this crime is so pitiless, so bestial, as truly to make the angels weep. [*Sotto voce*] I ask that you find this defendant guilty as charged. "

"Big Brother is watching you"

Client/juror/witness age range: All ages

Explanation: Arguably the most memorable line from George Orwell's novel *1984*.

Application: To draw a parallel between governmental invasion of privacy in Orwell's novel and similar governmental activity today.

Example: "Their phones were tapped. Their e-mail was read. Their home was searched. All these happened to our clients under the rubric of 'government security.' We maintain that there was no reasonable basis for any of these intrusions on their privacy. You know, some years ago in his novel *1984*, about a totalitarian state, George Orwell wrote, 'Big Brother is watching you.' Today, with advanced technology, it seems that Big Brother is alive and well, with all manner of means at his disposal to strip us of our privacy."

■ Catch-22

Client/juror/witness age range: All ages

Explanation: A difficult situation whose solution elements negate each other. From the 1961 novel *Catch-22* by Joseph Heller.

Application: To establish special circumstances when one is faced with a problem whose solution involves contradictory elements.

Example: "My client's mother was chronically sick, but they had no medical insurance. To get enough money to care for her, he needed a degree. But to afford the tuition to get a degree, he needed the money from a job that required a degree. He was in a classic Catch-22 situation, where one element of the solution cancels out the other. He applied for a job at a company in a field in which he has expertise, told them he had a degree, and they hired him. And he has performed extremely well in his job. But now the company is charging him with defrauding them because he filled out a false application. I request that the charge be dropped; he has done everything required of him in the job—and more—and the fact that he doesn't have a degree should be moot."

■ Dracula

Client/juror/witness age range: All ages

Explanation: The predatory Transylvanian vampire in Bram Stoker's 1897 novel *Dracula*. The story has been adapted on the stage and numerous times in film, and the character has entered popular culture as a symbol of lurking evil.

Application: To show that someone's lust to satisfy an addiction can destroy the lives of others.

Example: "The defendant has an insatiable craving for [name the drug], and he has not stopped at anything to satisfy that lust—robbery, assault, and, in the case here, murder. He has become a drug Dracula, ruining the lives of others not for blood, but for [name the drug]. If there is a case that demonstrates society's need to separate criminals from the law-abiding public, surely this is it."

■ "The evil that men do lives after them"

Client/juror/witness age range: All ages

Explanation: A line in Shakespeare's *Julius Caesar*, Act III.

Application: To establish that a civil action can be brought even after an offender has died.

Example: "In this civil suit we seek money damages from the estate of the man who assaulted my client. In an attempted robbery, he broke my client's back and inflicted serious, permanent head injuries. As he drew a gun, the police arrived and shot him dead. But my client will be mentally and physically disabled for the rest of her life. As Shakespeare wrote in *Julius Caesar*, 'The evil that men do lives after them.' And so it is here. We ask for damages in the amount of [give the amount]."

◼ Frankenstein's monster

Client/juror/witness age range: All ages

Explanation: The creature created by scientist Victor Frankenstein in Mary Shelley's 1818 novel *Frankenstein*. The story has been adapted numerous times in film, on the stage, and on television, and the character has entered popular culture as a symbol of out-of-control destruction.

Application: To show that greed can create a snowball effect that can overwhelm, for example, a company.

Example: "As treasurer, the defendant was one of the most trusted officials of his company. But he wanted to live the high life, so he systematically siphoned off hundreds of thousands of dollars of the firm's funds to do it. In the process, he created for the company a fiscal Frankenstein's monster of enormous debt spinning out of financial control, so that now the firm is on the verge of bankruptcy. Let him find out what kind of high life he can experience in a prison cell."

■ "hoist with his own petard"

Client/juror/witness age range: All ages

Explanation: A line in Shakespeare's *Hamlet*, Act III.

Application: To show that someone was trapped by the very scheme he had intended for someone else.

Example: "The defendant here planned his moves carefully. He schemed to plant false evidence of lying by his immediate superior in order to get that person's job. But a copy of a memo he sent to another involved in the plot was mistakenly attached to an e-mail to his superior. End of plot, end of career. To quote Shakespeare in *Hamlet*, he was 'hoist with his own petard.'"

■ ". . . an idea whose time has come"

Client/juror/witness age range: All ages

Explanation: The full quote, "Nothing is as powerful as an idea whose time has come," is attributed to Victor Hugo.

Application: In a judicial sense, that a conviction is long overdue.

Example: "The defendant here—no stranger to the judicial system—is accused of fraud, corruption, and intimidation, among numerous other felonies. He has thus far avoided a conviction, but the evidence against him here is overwhelming. You know, the nineteenth-century French novelist Victor Hugo wrote, 'Nothing is as powerful as an idea whose time has come.' And we say here, 'Nothing is as inevitable as a conviction whose time has come.' Send this racketeer to the prison sentence he so richly deserves."

■ "A lie which is half a truth is ever the blackest of lies"

Client/juror/witness age range: All ages

Explanation: A quote from the poem "The Grandmother" by Alfred, Lord Tennyson.

Application: To show that half a truth can be more devastating than a total lie.

Example: "Justice—and honesty—are what we are about in our legal system. But the main witness for the prosecution has smeared honesty, and therefore justice, in his testimony. Despite having sworn to tell 'the truth, the whole truth, and nothing but the truth,' he has been selective with the truth, and thus, in effect, has tried to wield a sledgehammer to my client's case. Perhaps the

British poet Alfred, Lord Tennyson said it best in his 1864 poem 'The Grandmother': 'a lie which is half a truth is ever the blackest of lies.' We will expose this lying testimony and wither it in the cleanliness of truth."

■ "a man's home is his castle"

Client, juror, witness age range: All ages

Explanation: A statement by English barrister and judge Sir Edward Coke in Part Three of the *1628 Institutes of the Laws of England*.

Application: To establish that one's home should be safe from intrusion and exploitation.

Example: "These defendants broke into the home of their victim family and looted it of anything they thought they could use or sell. Then, to try to cover their crime, they burned the home down. Items from the home were later found in the possession of the defendants, and there is evidence that accelerants were used in many locations of what remains of the home. Thus they are guilty of both burglary and arson. You know, as far back as 1628, the noted English jurist Sir Edward Coke said, 'a man's home is his castle.' But this family's home is now a pile of ashes. Send these defendants to the fate they deserve."

■ "The mass of men lead lives of quiet desperation"

Client/juror/witness age range: All ages

Explanation: A statement by transcendental philosopher Henry David Thoreau in his 1854 book, *Walden*.

Application: To show that extreme suffering need not be physical.

Example: "My client gets three meals a day, has adequate clean clothing, and is well sheltered, albeit in a tiny room. He is not physically assaulted. But he is the victim of an insidious, deliberate form of torture known as solitary confinement, for he is a convict at [name the prison] and is deprived of human contact twenty-four hours every day. His mental state has deteriorated markedly because of the denial of this basic human need. Many years ago, the philosopher Henry David Thoreau wrote, 'The mass of men lead lives of quiet desperation.' This could not be more true in the case of my client. Torture should not be a condition of his imprisonment. Remove him from this quietly barbaric environment, or the state also becomes a criminal."

■ ". . . not with a bang but a whimper"

Client/juror/witness age range: All ages

Explanation: A line from T. S. Eliot's 1925 poem "The Hollow Men."

Application: To draw a parallel between how the world ends and how the life of an imprisoned murderer ends.

Example: "To call him a stalker is only the beginning of the story. He targeted young women and then attacked, raped, and slowly murdered them. His sadistic crimes are enough to make you sick. You know, some years ago the poet T. S. Eliot wrote, 'This is the way the world ends. Not with a bang but a whimper.' The criminal life of the defendant before you today was loud and violent. Since there is no death penalty in this state, we ask that he be sentenced to life in prison without parole. There his life would end—lonely, forgotten, and isolated—a fate far better than he deserves."

"The object of torture is torture"

Client/juror/witness age range: All ages

Explanation: A line from George Orwell's novel *1984*.

Application: To submit that sadism, or some other extralegal motivation, was involved in police or military interrogation of a detained person.

Example: "My client was deprived of sleep. He was interrogated for hours, without respite. He was stripped naked and kept that way for hours. And these are only some of the things the [police, military] did to him as a 'suspected terrorist.' When you give a government absolute power over an individual, as in this case, beware of the results, since the torturers—for that is what they are—often act as if the power is theirs personally. In his novel *1984*, George Orwell said, 'The object of torture is torture.' He was writing about a totalitarian state. In this case, we submit that civilized treatment should have been accorded during questioning rather than the arbitrary interrogation techniques of a totalitarian state."

■ Orwell on equality

Client/juror/witness age range: All ages

Explanation: In his satiric 1949 novel *Animal Farm*, George Orwell wrote, "All animals are equal, but some animals are more equal than others."

Application: To show that criteria in areas such as employment, job contracts, housing, and academic admissions can be nominally based on equality but actually favor one individual or group over others.

Example: "We maintain that the petitioner was in fact discriminated against, under cover of so-called equality. You know, some years ago, George Orwell, in his satiric novel *Animal Farm*, wrote, 'All animals are equal, but some animals are more equal than others.' Unfortunately, that's still true today among humans, in a country at least nominally dedicated to equality for all. We submit that the petitioner's request for [employment, admission, etc.] should be granted."

■ "Pardon one offense and you encourage the commission of many"

Client/juror/witness age range: All ages

Explanation: Maxim 750 of first century B.C. Roman philosopher Publilius Syrus.

Application: To encourage a conviction by warning that an acquittal would send a message of perilous permissiveness.

Example: "The evidence is overwhelming in this case. The defendant lured his victim to an isolated place and then raped, robbed, and beat her mercilessly. And now counsel asks for a suspended sentence because he is still a teenager. For a deliberate, preplanned crime such as this? What kind of message does that send? Many centuries ago, the Roman philosopher Publilius Syrus wrote, 'Pardon one offense and you encourage the commission of many.' That maxim remains true today. I ask that the maximum allowable penalty be imposed on this vicious brute."

■ "Parting is such sweet sorrow"

Client/juror/witness age range: All ages

Explanation: A line in Shakespeare's *Romeo and Juliet*, Act II.

Application: To contrast the bittersweet sentiment of Shakespeare's statement with the simply bitter fact of prison life.

Example: "[First name of the defendant]'s fate is in your hands. The evidence shows that he was nowhere near where someone killed the victim. [First name of the defendant] is himself a victim, of mistaken identity. He is a family man and a solid member of this community. You know, Shakespeare said, 'Parting is such sweet sorrow'—but he was talking about seeing the person *the next day*. Please don't make [first name of the defendant]'s case a tragedy. Parting from his loved ones for prison would be unmitigated sorrow."

■ Polybius on conscience

Client/juror/witness age range: All ages

Explanation: "There is no witness so dreadful, no accuser so terrible as the conscience that dwells in the heart of every man," a statement by second century B.C. Greek historian Polybius in his *History*, Book XVIII.

Application: To mitigate the guilt of a client whose conscientious return of taken funds preceded any charge against him.

Example: "On Friday, my client needed money for expensive medication for his sick daughter. He is one of the 'working poor,' and no one would lend him the money

114

then. He closed up the store where he worked and took the money from the cash register, with the intention of somehow returning it on Monday morning. He bought the medication for his daughter on Friday and later that weekend got the money amount from a loan shark. On Monday, as he was about to return the money amount, he was confronted by his employer, who called the police, who arrested him for the theft. He has admitted the theft; he is a good man who did a technically bad thing. His conscience led him; as the Greek historian Polybius wrote many centuries ago, 'There is no witness so dreadful, no accuser so terrible as the conscience that dwells in the heart of every man.' If the charge will not be dropped, I ask that my client be given a suspended sentence for what is really a nominal crime."

■ "Power tends to corrupt; absolute power corrupts absolutely"

Client/juror/witness age range: All ages

Explanation: A statement of English historian Lord Acton (John Emerich Dalberg Acton), in a letter to Bishop Mandell Creighton in 1887.

Application: To illustrate that the exercise of power can be taken to gross extremes by those who wield it.

Example: "My clients are young and Arab. [Give the name of one of the clients] was driving his car; his three

Arab companions were passengers; all were smoking legal cigarettes. The car was stopped by two police officers who said they suspected marijuana possession. They searched the car, found no illegal substances, but did find four revolvers. My clients were arrested as 'suspected terrorists' even though all four men are licensed to carry firearms. They were taken to the police station, interrogated for days, deprived of sleep, stripped naked, and lied to in an attempt to extract a 'confession.' You know, some years ago English historian Lord Acton wrote, 'Power tends to corrupt; absolute power corrupts absolutely.' I think that the truth of this statement is blatantly illustrated by the absolute, arbitrary power the police wielded over these innocent men. I ask that they be released for lack of credible evidence of any crime."

■ "She speaks, yet she says nothing"

Client/juror/witness age range: All ages

Explanation: A line in Shakespeare's *Romeo and Juliet*, Act II.

Application: To denigrate the testimony of opposing counsel's witness.

Example: "Counsel's chief witness, the person on whose testimony his case principally rests, was really a nonwitness. Her statements were so imprecise, her recollections so fuzzy, as to make her testimony meaningless. As Shakespeare wrote in *Romeo and Juliet*, 'She speaks, yet she says nothing.'"

"...strength without justice is tyrannical"

Client/juror/witness age range: All ages

Explanation: A quote, published in 1670, from the *Pensées* by the seventeenth-century French writer and philosopher Blaise Pascal.

Application: To show that strength can delay or even deny justice.

Example: "My client's case against the respondent, a megacorporation, has dragged on for years. He suffered grievous bodily injury as an employee of the corporation, but his legal and medical expenses have been crushing, while the corporation's legal expenses have barely been noticed through the appeals. Thus we are taking his case pro bono—free—because we want to see justice done. You know, the seventeenth-century French writer and philosopher Blaise Pascal summed it up in his *Pensées*: 'strength without justice is tyrannical.'"

■ "There's small choice in rotten apples"

Client/juror/witness age range: All ages

Explanation: A line in Shakespeare's *The Taming of the Shrew*, Act I.

Application: To establish that a whistle-blower had no choice but to report a company's illegal activities to the authorities.

Example: "[The chief witness for the prosecution], when working for this defendant company, saw a pattern of corruption—bribe-taking, payoffs, skimming—to boggle the mind. She found it so pervasive that she found no one in the company to even listen to her about it, and she reported these illegal activities to the authorities. You know, Shakespeare, in *The Taming of the Shrew*, said, 'There's small choice in rotten apples.' And I ask that you tame these rotten apples by throwing them in a prison cell."

■ Trojan horse

Client/juror/witness age range: All ages

Explanation: As described by the ancient Roman poet Virgil in his epic poem *The Aeneid*, a hollow wooden horse covertly filled with Greek soldiers was brought into the city of Troy; the Greeks used these soldiers to defeat the Trojans.

Application: To emphasize that criminal ends can be achieved by hidden means.

Example: "Some criminals will stop at nothing to achieve what they want. In this case, the defendant used insider information gotten at the company where he was employed to defraud the company. He then sold the information to the company's competitors. Some of you will remember the Trojan horse—an invasive subterfuge used to defeat an enemy—in the Roman poet Virgil's *Aeneid*. That's what this defendant before us was—a Trojan horse. And nobody knew about it. Until now. Send this corporate traitor where what he is will be no secret—prison."

■ "Truth never yet fell dead"

Client/juror/witness age range: All ages

Explanation: A statement by theologian and social reformer Theodore Parker in *A Discourse on Matters Pertaining to Religion.*

Application: To show that the truth survives even when there is a fatality.

Example: "You have been impaneled to determine the facts in this case—the truth. The victim's throat was cut and he was robbed. Those facts are not disputed. You know, back in the nineteenth century, theologian and social reformer Theodore Parker wrote, 'Truth never yet fell dead.' The victim is dead but truth survives, and we submit that testimony and other evidence in this case will show that the defendant in fact committed these crimes."

■ "Weakness is not in your word"

Client/juror/witness age range: All ages

Explanation: A line from the poem "Rugby Chapel" (1867) by the English poet and critic Matthew Arnold.

Application: To neutralize opposing counsel's articulateness by attacking his case, not his presentation.

Example: "Opposing counsel is indeed articulate; he has a way with the English language. Let me quote another learned man, English poet and critic Matthew Arnold, who wrote, 'Weakness is not in your word.' And so say I. But ladies and gentlemen of the jury, please distinguish between presentation and substance. As jurors you are charged with judging the facts of the case, not their presentation."

■ ". . . where wealth accumulates, and men decay"

Client/juror/witness age range: All ages

Explanation: A quotation from the 1770 poem "The Deserted Village" by Oliver Goldsmith.

Application: To show the contrast between wealth accumulation and human decadence.

Example: "The company was enormously successful. They accumulated riches untold. But the legal riches of its money managers did not exactly rise to that level, for they siphoned off large chunks of that money for their personal use. Perhaps the Irish writer Oliver Goldsmith said it best in his 1770 poem 'The Deserted Village': 'Ill fares the land, to hastening ills a prey, where wealth accumulates, and men decay.' These managers accumulated the financial wealth, but they were decadent legally."

◼ "You can't make a silk purse out of a sow's ear"

Client/juror/witness age range: All ages

Explanation: A line from *Polite Conversation* by seventeenth-century English author Jonathan Swift.

Application: To establish that opposing counsel's case is devoid of merit.

Example: "Opposing counsel has tried hard. He has a weak case whose merit is just not appealing. You know, years ago English author Jonathan Swift said, 'You can't make a silk purse out of a sow's ear.' And that, I submit, is true of opposing counsel's case today."

■ "You cause what you abuse"

Client/juror/witness age range: All ages

Explanation: A statement by Juana Inés de la Cruz, a seventeenth-century Mexican nun, lyric poet, and early feminist, in *Hombres Necios* (Foolish Men).

Application: To establish that child abuse can lead to criminal activity by the abused child.

Example: "The home of these parents is filthy, their child shows signs of abuse, and both parents are on drugs. To make matters worse, the child himself, now a teenager, is on drugs and has been arrested for petty larceny. You know, more than three hundred years ago, Juana Inés de la Cruz, a Mexican nun, lyric poet, and early feminist, wrote, 'You cause what you abuse.' That statement is as true today as it was then. We submit that custody of this child be transferred from the parents to the court [or other appropriate party]."

Chapter 8
Sports

■ beanball

Client/juror/witness age range: All ages

Explanation: In baseball, a pitch thrown at a batter's head.

Application: To draw a parallel between a dangerous act in baseball and one in the business sphere.

Example: "The defendant in this case put others at peril by taking payoffs for not inspecting buildings properly. He let pass structural flaws that could cause sections of the building to collapse, resulting in serious injury or even death. You know, in baseball some unscrupulous pitchers throw a beanball—a dangerous pitch aimed at a batter's head—to intimidate, to get ahead. Well, in this case the defendant in effect threw an inspection beanball, putting others at grave risk to advance his own interests."

■ Black Sox

Client/juror/witness age range: All ages

Explanation: The 1919 Chicago White Sox; several members of the team took payoffs to lose the World Series that year.

Application: To compare the Black Sox, whose fans relied on them to do their best, with public or other officials who betrayed trust for selfish purposes.

Example: "How low can some people sink? These defendants—public officials, mind you—siphoned off funds meant for antipoverty programs in our community. The poor, children, the weak, the helpless relied on these funds, but they were stolen. This betrayal of trust reminds me of the infamous Black Sox—the 1919 Chicago White Sox—who took money to throw the World Series. And in so doing, they dashed the hopes of kids and other fans who relied on them to give an honest effort."

■ blitz

Client/juror/witness age range: All ages

Explanation: In football, intense pursuit of the passer by several members of the defensive team.

Application: To contrast legal violence, as in contact sports, with illegal, even murderous violence.

Example: "You know, football fans are familiar with the blitz—the defensive backs, ends, and linebackers chase the passer, to tackle him before he can pass the ball. It's very physical, but it's within the rules, and if they're too rough, they're penalized. But we have a very different kind of blitz here. These defendants—this gang of cowardly brutes—chased a lone young woman, the victim in this case, on her way home from work, raped her repeatedly, broke both her arms and legs and her backbone, smashed her skull in, and then threw her twisted corpse into a garbage pit. In football, you are penalized fifteen yards for unnecessary roughness. We leave it to the court, and to you, to decide what these vicious murderers deserve."

■ blown save

Client/juror/witness age range: All ages

Explanation: In baseball, when a relief pitcher fails to protect his team's lead in the final inning or innings.

Application: To draw a parallel between failure in sports and failure in business.

Example: "The claimant alleges that this company had no proper basis to terminate his employment. The facts show otherwise. He was responsible for checking, before a contract was finalized, that all the appropriate regulations were adhered to and all the paperwork was in order in a timely fashion. But on numerous occasions he failed to do this—whether through tardiness, ignorance or misunderstanding of the regulations, or just plain sloppy work. You know, in baseball, if a closer doesn't finish the game successfully, it's called a blown save, and after a number of blown saves, he's no longer with the team. Well, this claimant blew a lot of contracts for this company, and he quite appropriately is no longer employed there."

■ bush league

Client/juror/witness age range: All ages

Explanation: A minor or other inferior league in baseball; by extension, any inferior business or other activity.

Application: To compare inferior play in baseball with an inferior business operation.

Example: "The defendants in this case put out a prospectus that pictured them as running a first-class company, one that would reward its stockholders handsomely. But the company collapsed, and the stockholders were left holding the bag—an empty one. To draw a baseball analogy, their 'first-class company' was nothing more than bush league—inferior and substandard."

designated hitter

Client/juror/witness age range: All ages

Explanation: In baseball, a player with hitting skill selected by a team's manager to bat for the pitcher without causing the pitcher to be removed from the game.

Application: To contrast the lawful use of a bat in baseball—or by extension, the lawful use of any implement—with its illegal use in a crime.

Example: "You know, in baseball a designated hitter is chosen by the manager to bat for the pitcher because he can really smash the ball with that bat—sometimes so hard it lands in the stands for a home run, part of our wholesome, healthy national pastime. Well, there is another kind of designated hitter, the defendant in this courtroom. He also used a baseball bat—designated to do so by his gang leader, who told him to use it to smash the skull of [name the victim]. And he was quite successful—[name the victim] is now in [name the cemetery]."

■ get to first base

Client/juror/witness age range: All ages

Explanation: In baseball, the first stage in scoring a run; by extension, the first step in any course of action.

Application: To draw a parallel between this baseball term and other areas of life.

Example: "The defendant is a person of limited occupational talents. But he worked for a company with high skills standards, and couldn't get to first base on talent in that company. So he resorted to threats, intimidation, blackmail—anything to get ahead in the company, if not by skill, then by coercion."

■ left runners in scoring position

Client/juror/witness age range: All ages

Explanation: In baseball, a batter who did not drive runners home from second or third base, or a pitcher who left such runners stranded there.

Application: To analogize near-success in sports with that in business.

Example: "The claimant, a sales representative, says that he was improperly dismissed by this company. But in fact his sales record was poor; in particular, he failed to close the deal in numerous cases. To draw a baseball analogy, it is like a batter who leaves runners in scoring position—close, but no runs are scored."

out of left field

Client/juror/witness age range: All ages

Explanation: An unexpected or surprising development; the phrase has a baseball origin.

Application: Usable to expose a sudden, unanticipated strategy used in an attempt to demean one's client's character or reputation or to undermine his case or interests.

Example: "Claims of malfeasance against my client [the defendant] came out of left field. They were made suddenly, have no basis in fact, and were made by those who would profit by my client's leaving the company."

power play

Client/juror/witness age range: All ages

Explanation: In hockey, a one- or two-man advantage a team enjoys when a member of the opposing team is in the penalty box for a rules infraction.

Application: To draw a parallel between a legal advantage in sports and a criminal advantage.

Example: "Everyone likes an advantage. That's okay if it's according to the rules. For example, in hockey a team can play with one or even two more men on the ice if players on the other team have done something against the rules. Both teams know the rules and should play by them. But in the case before us, these vicious muggers, these defendants, observing no rules, had a power play of their own. With a six-to-one advantage, they jumped their victim and beat him senseless before robbing him."

■ quarterback

Client/juror/witness age range: All ages

Explanation: In football, the player who directs the offensive play of the team.

Application: To draw a parallel between leadership in sports and leadership in other areas, such as business.

Example: "I can personally vouch that [give the name], as president of the company, led it expertly and efficiently. He was, in effect, the quarterback of the company's operations. And like any good quarterback, he knew the resources he had and used them wisely, valued the competition's capabilities, and developed strategies to counter their moves."

■ red zone

Client/juror/witness age range: All ages

Explanation: In football, the area inside an opponent's twenty-yard line.

Application: Usable symbolically to portray impending peril (for a company or individual being attacked) or victory (for the attackers).

Example: "The corporate raiders were poised to strike. In football terms, it was the end of the game and they were in the company's red zone, about to strike the deathblow. The defendant in this case knew this, but it was privileged, *insider* information. And on the basis of this information, he illegally dumped his shares in the company before they plummeted."

■ replay

Client/juror/witness age range: All ages

Explanation: In sports, reviewing an official's on-field decision electronically to determine if the call was accurate.

Application: To emphasize to a jury the importance of reviewing the evidence before deciding which party prevails.

Example: "This is a complicated case. The evidence is enormous, and you, as judges of the facts, are tasked with evaluating it. Be sure to, in effect, replay the evidence in your mind or ask the court to let you review relevant material. You know, in sports, I'm sure many of you—and I—have seen on TV umpires' or referees' decisions overturned after the calls have been reviewed via electronic replay. The point is to get it right. But we submit that after you review the evidence, you will find for my client, that you will get it right."

■ sacking the quarterback

Client/juror/witness age range: All ages

Explanation: The tackling of the quarterback in football.

Application: To draw a parallel between the violent, sometimes vicious downing of a football quarterback and the symbolically violent, sometimes brutal ouster of a leader in the corporate sphere.

Example: "[My client] had an exemplary record of leading his company. Yet after the hostile takeover of the company, no football quarterback was sacked more viciously, more pitilessly than he by the new board members. Not only did they oust him from the company, they now are also trying to illegally strip him of the vast majority of benefits to which he is entitled from that company."

■ slam dunk

Client/juror/witness age range: All ages

Explanation: In basketball, an easy, close-in shot; by extension, a sure thing.

Application: To contrast a legal sure thing with an illegal act.

Example: "The defendant [or respondent] in this case had it made. A longtime employee of this company, he was head of its sales department, was well thought of, and was about to retire with a comfortable pension. Was his situation favorable? It was, as they say in basketball, a slam dunk. But not in his mind. He had been passed over for a vice presidency, with its stock options, and he was resentful. So he rigged the company's sales figures upward so he would get the attendant bonus under the company's rules. But he was entitled to no such bonus. He was, in fact, a thief."

■ sudden death

Client/juror/witness age range: All ages

Explanation: In football and hockey, the instant defeat of a team when the opposing team scores first in an overtime period.

Application: To use the term in a parallel sense with a homicide.

Example: "This was no ordinary mugging; this defendant was too cowardly for that. He killed his victim instantly, from behind, so there would be no noise, before robbing the corpse. You know, in football and hockey, we have sudden death, when one team defeats the other by scoring first in an overtime period. But that's playing by the rules of the game, and after the game, the teams shake hands. But this vicious killer, this defendant, was playing no game and observing no rules. The death he dealt was sudden and final."

Chapter 9

Millennial

■ "Beautiful Liar"

Client/juror/witness age range: All ages

Explanation: A song recorded by Beyoncé and Shakira in 2007.

Application: To show the value of cooperation in combating something that is superficially attractive but ultimately destructive to one's best interests.

Example: "It's heartwarming when you see two erstwhile competitors working together to leave someone who has been exploiting them. Such is true in this case; my clients, arrested for crack cocaine possession, competed in providing sex and money to a dealer to maintain their drug habit. Now they are clean and have reported the dealer to the authorities. It brings to mind Beyoncé and Shakira's 2007 hit song 'Beautiful Liar,' about two women who decided not to end their friendship after they dumped the seductive lover who had been cheating on both of them. My clients also did the right thing, and I ask that this be taken into account in deciding their fate in this case."

■ Bernie Madoff

Client/juror/witness age range: All ages

Explanation: In 2009, investment manager Bernard Madoff was convicted of investment fraud for using a Ponzi scheme.

Application: To draw a parallel between a convicted criminal and a current defendant.

Example: "This defendant is a thief. Period. But the people he defrauded didn't realize it until too late. Remember Bernie Madoff, the former 'adviser' convicted of investment fraud using a Ponzi scheme? He bilked thousands of investors of billions of dollars. Well, this defendant wasn't quite as wide-ranging as Bernie, but he did con dozens of people out of millions of dollars, some of their life savings, and using the same type of Ponzi scheme. Have him join Bernie in federal prison."

■ the Boston Marathon bombings

Client/juror/witness age range: All ages

Explanation: The terrorist explosions of April 15, 2013, at the finish line of the Boston Marathon; three were killed and some 264 were injured.

Application: To draw a parallel between violence with a political motive and that with an economic motive.

Example: "Their plan was well thought out. These defendants planted a timed bomb in a wastebasket at one end of [name a jewelry or other high-end merchandise] store. The explosion killed two customers and injured five. In the resulting confusion, the bombers, at the other end of the store, stole thousands of dollars' worth of [jewels, etc.] on display. Ladies and gentlemen, think Boston Marathon bombings, which killed three and injured hundreds. These defendants' motive was economic, not political, but the perpetrators were just as cowardly, just as contemptuous of human life, as at the marathon. Justice is needed, ladies and gentlemen. Justice!"

■ butterfly ballot

Client/juror/witness age range: All ages

Explanation: A ballot design considered by many to be confusing in the 2000 presidential voting in Florida.

Application: As a parallel to confusing labels or other instructions for foods, toys, appliances, or other items.

Example: "My client's child was severely injured as a result of using [name the manufacturer]'s toy. When my client assembled it, the so-called instructions that came with it were so confusing that a reasonably prudent person could not be expected to adequately understand them. It reminds me of the butterfly ballots in Florida in the 2000 presidential election. Remember? They were so confusing that a great many people didn't know who they were voting for."

■ cellcide

Client/juror/witness age range: All ages

Explanation: Death caused by a distracted driver's use of a cell phone.

Application: To name a destructive yet preventable event and thus to bring it to greater public attention.

Example: "The defendant was driving and using a cell phone simultaneously—a fatal combination here, for it resulted in the death of a seven-year-old girl when the defendant ran over her. You know, there's a new word for this, and I want you to remember it. It's called cellcide—cell, as in cell phone, and cide, as in homicide. The word was born in tragedy, yet lives on in preventable deaths such as this. For a cellcide is what this is—when using a phone while driving is more important than life itself."

■ DWB

Client/juror/witness age range: All ages

Explanation: Driving while black. The expression has come into increasing use in the twenty-first century.

Application: To establish that a driver was improperly stopped by the police because he was black.

Example: "My client did absolutely nothing improper, but the police *did*. His driving was flawless, but they stopped him. Then, when he reached in the glove compartment for his vehicle's registration, they shot him in the wrist. They later said they thought he was reaching for a gun. But there was no gun. None of this would have happened if my client had not been doing what is called DWB—driving while black."

global warming

Client/juror/witness age range: All ages

Explanation: A projected worldwide temperature rise that is allegedly due at least in part to actions by humans. The issue has come increasingly to the fore in the twenty-first century.

Application: To draw a parallel between lack of responsibility to prevent global warming and lack of responsibility to prevent a criminal occurrence.

Example: "Responsibility. What does it mean? It means we are to blame, or not to blame, for our own actions or lack of them. For example, if we as a society can prevent global warming, it is our responsibility to do so. But in the case before us, the defendant did not meet his responsibility to keep in good repair the brakes of the car he owned. The result was that he hit and killed a child while driving that car."

■ Hurricane Katrina

Client/juror/witness age range: All ages

Explanation: The highly destructive hurricane that ravaged New Orleans and the nearby Gulf Coast in 2005.

Application: To compare slow government response during and after Katrina with laggardly governmental action in other areas.

Example: "You know, this community [town, state] owes more to its senior citizens than it is delivering. 'The Greatest Generation' is getting older and sicker, and governmental programs have not kept pace. Government dragged its heels during and after Hurricane Katrina. Well, this is like Katrina in slow motion—inadequate nursing homes, or no homes, people in poverty or near-poverty, while government sits on its hands."

■ Indian Ocean tsunami of 2004

Client/juror/witness age range: All ages

Explanation: A monstrous series of waves that occurred with little or no warning and that caused widespread death, injuries, and destruction.

Application: To compare a tsunami—sudden and destructive—with a violent criminal attack.

Example: "They came seemingly out of nowhere. These defendants—these vicious brutes—who suddenly intruded on the victims in their home and raped, robbed, and murdered them. We have all seen on TV what a tsunami can do, such as the one that ravaged countries bordering the Indian Ocean in December 2004. Well, these thugs burst in on this family like a criminal tsunami—a tidal wave—and overwhelmed them before they had any chance to defend themselves."

Jerry Sandusky

Client/juror/witness age range: All ages

Explanation: In 2012, former football coach Jerry Sandusky was convicted of serial child molestation.

Application: To draw a parallel between a convicted criminal and a current defendant.

Example: "The defendant before you is guilty of the grossest form of child molestation. Remember Jerry Sandusky, who was convicted of molesting children when he was at Penn State? Well, this defendant was worse. The evidence that will be presented to you in this case is enough to make you sick. Vulnerable and defenseless youngsters were the targets of his lustful assaults. We urge you to find this sexual scourge guilty on all counts and to remove him from civilized society."

◼ 9/11

Client/juror/witness age range: All ages

Explanation: One of the most tragic dates in American history: the World Trade Center and Pentagon attacks.

Application: To equate in terms of criminality the attacks of September 11, 2001, with the date of a particular murder.

Example: "September 11—the date of the attacks on the World Trade Center and the Pentagon—are etched in the memories of Americans. And yet there is another date—[give it]—just as searing to some people in this courtroom. For that is the day their [spouse, son, brother, etc.] was brutally, senselessly, savagely murdered by the defendant on trial here. A nation mourned on September 11. And now these survivors will mourn for the rest of their lives on [date] for a murder equally as criminal, equally as barbaric."

◼ "No Surprise"

Client/juror/witness age range: All ages

Explanation: A 2009 song by the rock band Doughtry.

Application: To show that actions or circumstances often lead to predictable results.

Example: "As the chief financial officer of the company for which he worked, the defendant wielded enormous fiscal power. And he used it—to his own advantage. Remember Daughtry's song 'No Surprise'? It's about the end of a relationship. But in this case we have another end—that of the defendant's company, which went bankrupt—and that, ladies and gentlemen, is no surprise either. Because the defendant cooked the books, rifled the finances, and cheated the shareholders—all to support his lavish lifestyle. Send him to prison, where the bleak walls of his cell will be no surprise to him."

■ Osama bin Laden

Client/juror/witness age range: All ages

Explanation: The founder and, until his death in 2011, the leader of the terrorist organization al-Qaeda. He was the mastermind behind the 9/11 and other al-Qaeda attacks.

Application: To draw a parallel between notorious criminals who use stealth to attack and intimidate their enemies.

Example: "The defendant before us is a vicious drug overlord who has used any means necessary, by sneak attacks, to silence, intimidate, and assassinate those who oppose him. He is nothing less than a drug cartel version of Osama bin Laden, the head of Al-Qaeda who launched the 9/11 and other terrorist attacks. Ladies and gentlemen, I urge that you recommend the same terminal punishment to this drug beast that the United States meted out to bin Laden in 2011."

Pope Francis

Client/juror/witness age range: All ages

Explanation: The 266th Roman Catholic pontiff, Pope Francis—born Jorge Mario Bergoglio—has, since his elevation to the papacy in 2013, inspired many around the world, non-Catholics as well as Catholics, for his concern for the poor.

Application: To establish the character of a client by drawing a parallel between him and Pope Francis.

Example: "My client has been accused of siphoning off contributions to the poor for his own use. Nothing could be farther from the truth, and we will account for every penny. When you think of my client, think of Pope Francis—for the parallel is there, of devotion to relieving the suffering of the poor among us."

■ "Sometimes You Can't Make It on Your Own"

Client/juror/witness age range: All ages

Explanation: A song by U2 that won a Grammy for Song of the Year in 2006.

Application: To draw a parallel between the song's title and the fact that a defendant's fate is in the hands of the jury.

Example: "You know, [my client] has been very open and forthcoming. She has testified and undergone cross-examination when she wasn't required to, and we maintain that there is no case against her. She has done all she can. You know, U2 recorded a song that won a Grammy in 2006, 'Sometimes You Can't Make It on Your Own.' And that's what we say to you now. Her fate is up to you. I ask that you look at all the evidence and find [first name of the defendant] not guilty."

■ texting

Client/juror/witness age range: All ages

Explanation: An electronic communication procedure; its overuse has been likened to an addiction.

Application: To show that abuse of an otherwise benign practice can have deleterious results.

146

Example: "The defendant, a nineteen-year-old, is a chronic texter—hundreds of times a day. A harmless addiction, you might say? Not here. He was texting while driving—with the result that he plowed into the victim in this case, who has suffered multiple fractures and other injuries. He will never walk again. I strongly urge that you convict this defendant accordingly."

■ Tiger Woods

Client/juror/witness age range: All ages

Explanation: Eldrick Tont ("Tiger") Woods is widely regarded as one of the best golfers of all time, but he has acknowledged mistakes in his personal life.

Application: To establish that one should be judged on the basis of his qualifications, not on extraneous matters.

Example: "In this case I urge that you judge my client on the basis of his professional performance, not on his personal problems. Let me draw a Tiger Woods analogy. On the golf course, Tiger is not penalized strokes because of his admitted indiscretions in his private life; rather he is judged on how well he plays golf. The same standard—professional over personal life—applies here."

■ "You Can't Have That"

Client/juror/witness age range: All ages

Explanation: A 2001 recording by JD Blu Band.

Application: This song title itself could be used to directly counter opposing counsel's case.

Example: "You have used your company's assets for your own private gain; you have cheated the stockholders and your partners. Well, Mr. Defendant, the title of a single by JD Blu Band in 2001 sums up what we say to you now: 'You Can't Have That'!"